MW00782205

Presented to: _____

by: _____

Date: _____

The Ways of Elvis

Enjoy the stories

My best,

John Dawson

The Ways of Elvis
Lessons from His Life

John Dawson

Tapestry Press
Irving, Texas

Tapestry Press
3649 Conflans Road
Suite 103
Irving, TX 75061

Printed in the U.S.A.
06 05 04 03 02   1 2 3 4 5

Library of Congress Cataloging-in-Publication Data
ISBN 1-930819-21-8

PHOTO CREDITS:
James Burton International Fan Club – page 34
John Dawson – pages xi, xvi, 1, 3, 16, 21, 30, 49, 52, 82, 84
Sean Shaver – page 15
"Max"ene Shields – page 32
Jim Stout – cover photo, pages 25, 40, 46, 56, 62, 69, 76
Rachel Tyre – page 17

Layout by
D. & F. Scott Publishing, Inc.
N. Richland Hills, Texas

To my wife, Christy, for her loving support
To my daughter, Faith, for all the joy she has brought me
To my son, Andrew, for striving towards his goals
To my parents for teaching me to never give up

Contents

Foreword

I t is often difficult for me to talk and write about Elvis without feeling emotional. I miss him so much. In 1960, my mother, Dee Stanley, married Elvis Presley's father, Vernon.

I was four years old when we moved into the Graceland mansion. Elvis wasn't just an entertainer in my eyes; he had become my big brother. Over the next seventeen years, Elvis was my stepbrother, my friend, my mentor, and later, my boss. I don't boast that I knew Elvis better than anyone else, because I didn't. But I did know him well.

As a family member and employee, I had unique opportunities to be with Elvis during holidays, on back lots of movie studios, at recording sessions, on television specials, and hundreds of concerts. At seventeen, I went to work for Elvis as a personal aide and bodyguard and witnessed many phases of his life both personally and professionally. I was with him until his untimely death on August 16, 1977.

I have always wanted people to know the Elvis I knew. Not just Elvis the superstar, but Elvis the human being. This book introduces you to the man. It is not just for Elvis's fans, but is also for those who are curious about Elvis's phenomenal popularity twenty-five years after his death. His ways. His words. Every quote that my friend John Dawson transcribed is from Elvis himself, from actual recordings of press conferences, concerts, and handwritten notes. He has spent years researching and compiling this material.

There are many valuable things you can learn from Elvis: the importance of goal setting, confidence, and hard work; having good management and employees you can depend on; making time for your family; being a good friend; taking time off for recreation; helping the less fortunate; being respectful to people; and walking with the Lord. These are the key elements to Elvis's life and longevity.

Elvis once said, "David, I've taught you everything you know, but not everything I know." It's been almost twenty-five years since I last spoke to him and I'm still learning from his ways. Through John Dawson's *The Ways of Elvis*, now, like me, you can treasure your moments with Elvis.

David E. Stanley

Acknowledgments

I am indebted to the following for their assistance and support over the years: First, I would like to thank my family; my beautiful wife Christy for her love and belief in me; my children Andrew and Faith, for their love and understanding; my brother Mike Dawson, for always being there; my sister-in-law Terry Dawson, for her encouragement; Nina and Jim Puckett, for taking me to my only Elvis concert; David Stanley, for his love and devotion to his stepbrother Elvis, and for his many years of friendship; Lynn Stanley, for her prayers; Larry Patrick, for his friendship and many years of sharing Elvis collectibles; James Burton, my favorite guitarist and friend; Elvis Presley Enterprises, for keeping Elvis's memory alive; Patsy Anderson, for shepherding the fans; Jimmy Stout, for his beautiful Elvis photos; Rachel Tyre, for her Elvis photo; Sean Shaver, for his friendship and for sharing his gorgeous Elvis photos; "Max"ene Shields, for her Elvis influence and photos; Wendell Hawkins, for sharing his records; Priscilla Presley, for always being kind to me; Lisa Marie Presley, for her love for her father and charitable works; Charlie Hodge; Lamar Fike, for many fun times; Jimmy Velvet, for his friendship and hospitality over the years; Sylvia Corley, of the James Burton International Fan Club, P.O. Box 61475, Jacksonville Beach, FL 32240, for her years of sharing; Steve and Cathy Curtis, for their support and love for Elvis; my TCB Elvis Style Fan Club family; Christopher Lovett, for his cover design and computer skills; my in-laws Tom and Mary Banks, for giving me a quiet and inspirational place to write; Tommy, Jenny, Ben, Kelly, and Andy Rogers, for their love and support; Dan Poynter, for his publishing knowledge; Dottie Walters, for her encouragement and expertise; and Elvis, for the years of enjoyment and motivation.

Disclaimer

This book is designed to provide information about the subject matter covered. It is sold with the understanding that the publisher and authors are not engaged in rendering legal, accounting, or other professional services. If legal or other expert assistance is required, the services of a competent professional should be sought.

It is not the purpose of this manual to reprint all the information that is otherwise available on Elvis Presley or self-help, but to complement, amplify, and supplement other texts.

Modeling yourself after Elvis's successes is not a quick fix to a new you. Anyone wishing to make self-improvement in any area must expect to invest time and effort without any guarantee of success. Only you can improve yourself. It is imperative that you desire a change.

All quotes used in this book were transcribed directly from numerous press conferences, concerts, and home recordings. Every effort has been made to make this book as complete and accurate as possible. However, there may be mistakes both typographical and in content. Therefore, the text should be used only as a general guide and not as the ultimate resource book on the life of Elvis Presley or as a cure-all for behavioral modification.

The purpose of this manual is to educate and entertain. The author and/or publisher shall have neither liability nor responsibility to any person or entity with respect to any loss or damage caused or alleged to be caused directly or indirectly by the information contained in this book. Elvis, Elvis Presley, and TCB are registered trademarks of Elvis Presley Enterprises, Inc.

A Word from the Author

Forget what you have heard about Elvis's life, music, and legend. Your Elvis knowledge is about to change—for the better! Now you will understand why Elvis is worth remembering and how he came to be one of the most influential people of the twentieth century and is becoming a sustaining force in the twenty-first century. You will discover how to model his techniques to make your dreams come true.

Almost everyone wants to be successful, whether in being successful in business, relationships, sports, healthwise, or otherwise. People think about it. They dream about it. They talk about it. Sadly, very few achieve their ambitions in life.

Elvis, like us all, had imperfections. It is not my intent to paint him as a demigod of perfection. But lessons can also be learned from some of the bad choices he made. Elvis Presley was a human being, but no one can argue the fact that Elvis was successful. He excelled and set precedents at almost everything he did. Elvis was original; he was larger than life.

I hope this book will explain to you how Elvis became one of the most beloved, recognized, and unexplainable phenomenons in the world even twenty-five years after his death and how you can apply the principles by which he lived personally and professionally to your life for self-improvement. Through Elvis's words and experiences, you too can rise above your circumstances and reach your goals.

It was from Elvis that I learned to say "ma'am" and "sir," not from my parental upbringing. I also discovered how to work hard, to dress sharp, to overcome shyness, to be loyal, to be sure of myself, and to feel confident talking to girls. Through Elvis I came to appreciate gospel music and the importance of walking with the Lord. Elvis had a way about him. He had common sense, good instincts, and a keen sense of humor. I asked myself; "What can I learn from this guy that has captivated audiences, common people, reporters, celebrities, military men, and presidents for more than fifty years?" Read on.

John Dawson, Hurst, Texas

About the Author

John Dawson has been an Elvis fan and collector since age twelve and a student of all that is Elvis for almost as long. A certified hypnotist and professional photographer, he has combined his interest in photography and Elvis to develop a collection of Elvis-related photographs.

He also has an extensive collection of Elvis's records, books, videos and other memorabilia. Dawson's photographs and Elvis collection have been seen on television's *A Current Affair*, *Geraldo*, *Evening Magazine*, and *Inside Edition*. He was a consultant on the videos *Life With Elvis* and *Elvis Week: Legacy of a Legend*. He was the consultant and Elvis scholar for the Fox Family Channel's two-hour documentary, "The Presleys: Rock' n' Roll Royalty" and was interviewed by Elvis Presley Enterprises fan relations manager, Patsy Anderson, last year for a Graceland production on Presley Place that featured Elvis's daughter Lisa Marie Presley.

Moreover, Dawson has served in the research, writing, and photographs on numerous books on Elvis, including: *Life With Elvis*; *Elvis: His Life From A to Z*; *The Elvis Encyclopedia*; *Raised On Rock*; *The Complete Idiot's Guide to Elvis*; and *Elvis Immortal*. He is the president of The Taking Care of Business Elvis Style Fan Club in Hurst, Texas.

John is a certified hypnotherapist and dynamic public speaker. He is the president and owner of Daily Doses of Hypnosis in Hurst, Texas, where he maintains a highly successful hypnosis practice. As a hypnotist, he has seen his clients accomplish amazing things by using the power of their minds to lose weight, quit smoking, manage stress, build confidence, and enhance sports and work performance.

Elvis Firsts

Elvis was the first rock 'n' roll movie star.

Elvis made the first music video.

Elvis was the first entertainer to be paid $50,000 for a single television appearance.

Elvis was the first recording artist to have a record go platinum in ten days.

Elvis was the first singer to have a million-selling record before it was officially released.

Elvis was the first movie star to make one million dollars a movie.

Elvis was the first entertainer to do a live show worldwide via satellite.

Elvis is the first entertainer to have more than 625 active fan clubs around the world.

Elvis is the first entertainer to do a world tour to sell out audiences after his death (via video footage).

Elvis is the first and only entertainer voted Artist of the Twentieth Century.

Elvis is the first recording artist to be a Hall of Famer in three music genres.

Elvis is the first and only recording artist who has sold more than one billion record units worldwide.

I was a dreamer. I read comic books and I was the hero of the comic book. I saw movies and I was the hero in the movie. So every dream that I ever dreamed has come true a hundred times.

—Elvis A. Presley

All That I Am
(Elvis on Himself)

On August 29, 1956, Elvis gave an interview for what would become a record entitled *The Truth About Me*. This record was an insert in a magazine called *Elvis Answers Back*. It took place during the height of Elvis's popularity and the controversy that followed his meteoric rise to fame:

> Hi, this is Elvis Presley. I guess the first thing people want to know is why I can't stand still when I'm singing. Some people tap their feet. Some people snap their fingers. And some people just sway back and forth. I just sort of do 'em all together, I guess. Singin' rhythm and blues really knocks it out. I watch my audience and listen to 'em, and I know that we're all getting something out of our system. None of

> us knows what it is. The important thing is that we're gettin' rid of it and nobody's gettin' hurt. In a lot of the mail I get, people ask questions about the kind of things I do and all sort of stuff. Well, I don't smoke and I don't drink, and I love to go to movies. Maybe someday I'm gonna have a home and a family of my own and I'm not gonna budge from it. I was an only child but maybe my kids won't be. I suppose this raises another question:

Am I in love? No. [laughs] I thought I been in love but I guess I wasn't. It just passed over. I guess I haven't met the girl yet, but I will. And I hope it won't be too long 'cause I get lonesome sometimes. I get lonesome right in the middle of a crowd. But I've got a feelin' that with her—whoever she may be—I won't be lonesome, no matter where I am. Well, thanks for letting me talk to you and sorta get things off of my chest. I sure appreciate you listening to my RCA Victor records, and I'd like to thank all the disc jockeys for playing 'em. Bye-bye.

∽

I'm not a loner, I don't think. But I've got to admit, sometimes I like just getting off by myself. You know. Just off somewhere alone. No crowds or anything. Where it's just peaceful. And quiet. And you can think.

In June of 1972, Elvis held a rare press conference in the wake of his first live concert appearances in New York. He sold out four concerts at Madison Square Garden. Elvis was relaxed and candid. One reporter asked him how close he came to living up to his image:

The image is one thing. The human being is another, you know. It's very hard to live up to an image. I'll put it that way.

In June of 1977, less than a month-and-a-half before his death, CBS filmed several shows from Elvis's last tour for a one-hour television special called *Elvis in Concert*. He was tired and didn't want to do the special, but he faced the music. During the opening of the concert he again admitted before his fans and television audience how nervous he was:

If you think I'm nervous, you're right.

Elvis's common sense and moral upbringing helped him to stay out of trouble as he discussed this issue with a reporter on March 24, 1956, in an interview at the Warrick Hotel:

> *I think I know right from wrong. You have to be careful out there. Everywhere. It's so easy to get into trouble. You can get trapped into something. It's so easy.*

Elvis was a deeply religious person. He was brought up in the Assembly of God church. That was where Elvis learned to sing. He always pondered the reason why he of all people had been chosen for such fame. Elvis felt that God played a hand in his popularity. Here, Elvis responds to a *TV Guide* reporter who used the term "Holy Roller" during an interview in 1956:

> *I have never used that expression. That's another deal. See, I belong to Assembly of God church, which is a holiness church. I was raised up in a little Assembly of God church, and some character called 'em Holy Rollers. And that's where that got started. I always attended church where people sang, stood up and sang in the choir, and worshiped God. I have never used the expression "Holy Roller."*

The Assembly of God Church that Elvis's family attended in Tupelo

Elvis was asked if he still attended church.

> *Every opportunity I get. I don't have as much opportunity as I used to, because I'm on the road most of the time.*

Later in 1956, Elvis responds to an article stating that fame had made him forget about religion:

> *I sat right down and cut that out of the paper and sent it home for my mama to put in my scrapbook. I expected they'd start saying things like that. About me not being religious, I mean—well, I'm not sure what they mean by "religious" in that article, but I can tell you this much. I don't think they're right in saying things like that. No, I don't go to church regular any more, if that's what they mean by religious. Being on the road all the time, and traveling every minute I'm not working, I can't ever be sure when I'll have a Sunday free to myself. I wish I could, just like I wish I could be with my folks more often, but I can't. So if they mean just going to church regularly makes you religious, then I guess I don't fit up to what they want. But I want you to know this. I believe in God. I believe in Him with all my heart. I believe all good things come from God. That includes all the good things that have come to me and to my folks. And the way I feel about it, being religious means that you love God and are real grateful for all He's given, and want to work for Him. I feel deep in my heart that I'm doing all this. And I pray that if I'm wrong in feeling the way I do, God will tell me, because I owe everything that's happened to me to Him.*

In a later interview, Elvis again mentions his religious convictions:

> *I've never even felt a change. The only thing I've felt is that—is happiness, that things have gotten better for me. That God has blessed me and that he's given me a lot of things that a lot of people would like to have, that I would like to see other people have. In other words, I wish that*

everybody could have, you know, luxuries in life, but I guess that's impossible . . . Well I don't attend church regularly or nothing like that, but I'm a true believer in God if that's what you mean. I believe that all good things come from God.

On January 16, 1971, Elvis was selected by the United States Junior Chamber of Commerce (Jaycees) as one of ten outstanding young men of America. It was the only award for which he made a public reception speech. During his talk he made reference to his fellow inductees building the kingdom of heaven:

And these gentlemen over here, you see these type people who care, that are dedicated. You realize that it's not impossible that they might be building the kingdom of Heaven. It's not too far-fetched from reality.

During a mid-1970s Las Vegas engagement, Elvis wrote a prayer to God:

I'll never smoke little cigars again. Pipe collection is just that, a collection, and for as strong as God can strengthen me, will never consciously or subconsciously do anything to endanger my voice or health. Never consciously or not do anything to upset the Lord thy God. Never to—[unintelligible]—my Father, my friend, or anyone else to be a friend to my body as long as I shall live. To love the Lord my God with all my heart, soul, and body or best as I can. To wish happiness for Priscilla, Mike, or parties involved. To hold no malice against no man as long as I live. With God's help be thankful for Col. Tom P., George, everyone who has helped me and will help me. To love and appreciate Linda with all my heart, and my body. To sing with the utmost of my ability and bring happiness thru singing and laughter, with love and with joy utmost of ability. My grandmother, all my employees, who have stood by me when the road was rough. All these and more I promise

> with God's help to uphold all these and many more as long
> as I shall live. They and I ask thru Christ our Lord to my
> God. Amen. As long as I shall live on this earth I solemnly
> swear with God's help to try to bring joy and happiness
> thru singing, thru the art of karate, Ed Parker and many
> more, to protect as myself a friend, loved one, God and
> country. With all my heart. E. P.

In 1972, during his famous Madison Square Garden press
conference he was asked what he thought about the current
music scene:

> Oh, I, I don't know. I really can't criticize anybody in the
> entertainment field. I think there's room for everybody. I
> hate to criticize another performer.

In 1972, Elvis was asked if he had any political ambitions:

> No, sir, I don't have any other aspirations in politics or any-
> thing of that nature. I'm not involved in that at all. I'm just
> an entertainer. Okay.

During a relaxed evening with friends in 1973, Elvis recited a
poem he had written:

> Did you hear the little poem that I wrote?
>
> As I awoke this morning
> When all sweet things are born
> A robin perched on my windowsill
> To greet the coming dawn
> He sang a song so sweetly
> And paused for a moment's lull
> I gently raised the window
> And crushed his fucking skull
>
> [laughter] Oh, Lord have mercy.

Being one of the most famous people in the world left Elvis particularly vulnerable to slander. During a Las Vegas performance in 1974, Elvis responded to rumors going around about him being "strung out" on drugs:

In this day and time you can't even get sick. You are strung out! Well by God, I'll tell you something, friend. I have never been strung out in my life; except on music. When I got sick, here in the hotel, I got sick here that one night, had a 102 temperature; they wouldn't let me perform. And from three different sources I heard I was strung out on heroin. I swear to God. Hotel employees, Jack, bellboys, freaks that carry your luggage up to the room, people working around, you know, talkin' maids; and I was sick, you know, had a doctor, had the flu, got over it in one day. But all across this town, I was strung out. So, I told them earlier; and don't you get offended, ladies and gentlemen, I'm talkin' to somebody else. If I find or hear the individual that has said that about me, I'm gonna break your goddamn neck! You son of a bitch! That is dangerous to myself, to my little daughter, to my father, to my friends, my doctor, to everybody, my relationship with you [his fans], my relationship up here on stage. I will pull your goddamn tongue out by the roots! Thank you very much.

Elvis always put his heart into his work. He loved sentimental love songs. After recording a take of *Blue Eyes Crying in the Rain* in 1976, Elvis made the following statement:

I get carried away very easily. Emotional son of a bitch.

In the 1950s, at the beginning of his career, Elvis received a lot of criticism for his stage movements. After his return to live performances in Las Vegas in 1969, Elvis made this quip:

People thought for a long time I was trying to be sexy and everything. I'm just trying to stand up.

Being one of the most famous entertainers in the world put Elvis on a pedestal for many people. During a Las Vegas performance, Elvis shared the following story explaining how human he really was:

> You'll never guess where I was when the intro [theme from 2001: A Space Odyssey] came on [laughs]. You talk about some fast movements [laughter]. Da, da, da, ch, ch, ch, you know, I'm in the bathroom. You know that's the first time that's ever happened to me [laughter]. I don't do things like that. That's what a woman said to me the other day. I went to a football game. Listen to this, went to a football game and a lady said, she asked a friend of mine, she said, "I hear Elvis Presley is here at the Decatur football game." And the fellow said, "Yeah." She said, "I hear he's staying in the press box." "Yes." She said, "I hear he's in the bathroom" [laughter]. He said, "Yeah." And the lady said very seriously, "I didn't think he did that." It's the truth. I swear to God.

Elvis was always aware of the impact he had on people. He knew it was important to keep the proper image. He expressed this during a 1956 interview:

> If there's anything I've tried to do, I've tried to live a straight, clean life and not set any bad example. You cannot please everyone.

Elvis gave a rather revealing one-on-one interview in 1962:

> What I look at myself as, not really playing everything down, but as a human being, really, who has been very, extremely fortunate—in so many ways. Although I have had and still have some very lonely. . . and you know. There are times when I really don't know, it feels like I don't know what I'm going to do next.

Like many people who have to speak publicly, Elvis would sometimes fumble for words. Here is an example of how he dealt with the situation before a live audience:

We did a song, went somin' like this, went somin' like this. Went something like this [whistles]. Whew! I can't understand myself, man, I don't know how you, mumbling. Boy, I tell ya that motor's hard to get to going tonight. If it ever goes it'll be . . . [laughs].

Elvis never forgot his country beginnings. He jokingly revealed this during a Las Vegas performance in the 1970s while trying to pronounce the word "something":

If I happen to miss somin', somin', whew, something. You know. You can take the boy out of the country, but . . .

During a 1970 Las Vegas appearance, Elvis joked about his image with his fans:

If I get my hair out of my eyes, I can see you out there, maybe. Of course, it would blow my image, but uh . . . it's been blown before . . . [laughter]. Image. Image. Say image [laughs]. Well, that's it, boy.

Elvis realized that his fans expected a certain type song and a highly charged performance from him. He expressed this during a Las Vegas engagement:

You know, a lot of times I wish I was the type performer like, you know, the guys that sing, Everybody Loves Somebody (from the Dean Martin song), but I can't do that. See, because people will come in here and say, "he can't move anymore," you know, so I have to get the "bod" moving whether I like it or not.

Elvis loved his fans and he never forgot that they made him who he was. He never had the police remove them from his property. He loved signing autographs. His relationship with his fans was one of the greatest love stories ever. During one of his 1970s concerts a policeman was being rude to the fans walking down for Elvis's scarves. Elvis reprimanded the officer:

> *Don't be so rough on the people when they come down here. They're just coming down to get scarves. Don't treat them like they're going to jail, goddamnit.*

Elvis was never ashamed to let his fans know he was human. He enjoyed sharing stories with them, and the fans loved for him to do that. Here, Elvis shared an instance regarding his first New Year's Eve concert when he played to the biggest audience of his career:

> *On January first of this year [1976], we played Pontiac, Michigan, in a place that holds sixty-four thousand people, which was one of the largest groups of people I'd ever played to. So, I never was so scared in my life. People ask me if I get nervous before I go on stage. You better believe it. I mean, uh, just before I go on stage, you could walk up to me and say, "Hey, your hair's on fire." I'd say, Yeah. Yeah. Anyway, the fourth song of the show my pants ripped. Happy New Year, everybody. And they had me up on this pedestal- type thing with everybody all around me, you know. So, I was like this [laughter], and luckily, they had another suit off stage or one off stage. Changed clothes, came back on and Charlie [Hodge] forgot what song was up next. We cut the show short. Okay. It got to be twenty seconds until midnight. I was supposed to do the countdown with everybody, you know. Anyway, they had a huge clock, right. Well, I couldn't see it because the spotlight was in my eyes, so this clock was in my eyes. See, I couldn't see it. There was twenty seconds, fifteen seconds, you know, one, two . . . backwards and finally, just five seconds before midnight they turned the lights off, and I could see the clock and I started counting with them. Everybody started singing* Auld Lang Syne. *Well, I didn't know*

the words to it [laughter], so I said, "May old acquaintance hmmm, hmmm, hmmm" and let the audience sing it. Okay they ended the first verse. I thought, "Well, that's it." No. There's a second verse to it. I don't believe it. So, uh, then I go back to Charlie, it's just after midnight. I said, "What song is up next!" He said, "Let's take it on home." We'd only been on stage for thirty minutes, you know. They would've killed us. And on top of that, other than that I supposedly got married last week to somebody. Naw, I just read it in the paper. I find out more stuff about myself in the paper than anything else.

Elvis shared a similar experience with another audience after busting the seat out of his pants again. He had a history of this from the time he returned to the stage in 1969:

I've got to confess something to you folks. When I bent over earlier I ripped the seat out of this suit. It's not that bad, is it! I'll just stand like this for the whole night, but it did go.

In December of 1976, Elvis sprained his ankle during what was to become his last Las Vegas engagement. The sprain hindered Elvis's physical movement. Elvis spent much of his show on a stool joking about not being able to play the guitar. In reality, he could play quite well. He demonstrated that fact during his 1968 "Elvis" NBC-TV special. He shared his thoughts during the rough times at work:

See, I had all those pictures taken years ago with a guitar. Strictly a front. I couldn't play the guitar. Just beat the day-lights out of it, you know. You watch. You watch and see what I mean. Now I'm out here with a bum leg . . . who knows what else will go wrong. I'll turn into a werewolf, I know it.

During his return to live performing in Las Vegas in 1969, Elvis joked about his wild stage antics:

> *They're going to put me away, man. I know, it's just a mat-*
> *ter of time.*

During his August 19, 1974, opening show Elvis jokingly
revealed moments of his personal life while singing the song
Good Time Charlie's Got the Blues:

> *"Play around you'll lose your wife," (I've already done that,)*
> *"Play too long you'll lose your life." (I almost did that.)*

Elvis described his mortality:

> *I look at myself strictly as a human being who's, like I said,*
> *has been very lucky, but whose life—I have blood running*
> *through my veins, and can be snuffed out in just a matter of*
> *seconds, and not as anything supernatural or better than*
> *any other human being.*

In 1970, an earthquake shook the International Hotel in Las
Vegas while Elvis was sleeping:

> *I'll tell you what, that International Hotel almost fell. That*
> *son of a bitch was rockin' back and forth . . . I swear to God.*
> *I went to bed at six o'clock in the morning, and Priscilla was*
> *there. I laid in bed and I thought "God almighty, what's*
> *goin' on here?" The bed was movin', see. So I got up and*
> *walked out in the hallway . . . had my flashlight and my gun*
> *in one hand. I looked at the big chandelier hangin' over the*
> *dining room table . . . that son of a bitch was shakin' man,*
> *back and forth. It was the weirdest feeling I ever had in my*
> *life. Well, I opened the door to see if the wind was blowing.*
> *No wind blowing. Well, I tell you what, it was the weirdest*
> *feelin' I ever had. 'Course that big hotel was movin' now,*
> *back and forth. It's supposed to move and that son of a bitch*
> *was doin' it, boy! I was ready to get out of that place, man. I*
> *was headin' for the elevator in my underwear [laughs]. That*
> *third show was gonna be a dilly, boy. [He was performing*
> *two shows a night.]*

Elvis talked about having glaucoma:

> *I told them to say "eye infection" 'cause that's what I wanted it to be. It was glaucoma, but it's gone. It's all cleared up. I'm out running around now.*

On July 5, 1975, Elvis played his hometown, Memphis, Tennessee, and he spoke to his fans about being hospitalized:

> *I'd like to tell you, ladies and gentlemen, since I was here last time, I was in the hospital for a couple of things. Nothing real serious. And I'm over that and I'm out working, and I'm glad to be back working again.*

Elvis believed the secret to living was giving. He supported countless charities throughout his life. In 1957, Elvis did a rare ad for the March of Dimes:

> *You know, so many kids and adults too have gotten one of the roughest breaks that can happen to a person. I'm talking about polio. Sure, we're on the way to conquering it, thanks to the Salk vaccine. But take it from me, it sure isn't licked yet. Right now, some eighty thousand polio victims need help. Some of them are paralyzed so they can't even move a finger. Others can't do the simplest, everyday things that we take so much for granted. But the situation isn't hopeless. We can help these people, and the way to do it is this: join the 1957 March of Dimes. Please. It's very urgent. Give every dime and dollar you can to this great cause.*

During a 1970s Las Vegas engagement Elvis told his audience about a fund-raiser that he and Colonel Parker had set up:

> *There's a few people in the audience I'd like to acknowledge. I don't know if you know this or not, but out front, Colonel Parker, my manager, set up a booth when we came here for the Heart Fund, you know, the American Heart Association, and they made me a member of the American*

Heart Association today. And thanks to you and the two weeks we've been here, they've raised $17,000.

During his Las Vegas show on August 11, 1970, Elvis cited this recitation written by Hank Williams before singing the song *Walk a Mile in My Shoes:*

There was a guy who said one time—he said: You never stood in that man's shoes, or saw the things through his eyes. Or stood and watched with helpless hands, while the heart inside you dies. So help your brother along the way, no matter where he starts. For the same God that made you made him too. These men with broken hearts. I'd like to sing a song along the same line.

That's All Right, Mama

(Elvis on Family)

Elvis was very family oriented. He loved having his family members around. He trusted them implicitly. He hired many of them to work for him. Elvis was particularly fond of his mother. He shared some rare comments about his mother in a Jack Bentley interview in 1962:

Charlie Stone, Elvis's stepbrother David Stanley, and Elvis at the end of a concert in 1977.

It's funny she never really wanted anything—you know, anything fancy. She just stayed the same all the way through the whole thing. I wish—you know, there's a lot of things that have happened since she passed that I wish she could have been around to see. It would have made her very happy and very proud, But that's life. I can't help it.

Elvis's pride and joy was his beautiful little girl Lisa Marie. He was so proud of her, he named his 880 Convair jet plane after her. Elvis loved to introduce her to his audiences when she was able to attend his concerts. On November 15, 1972, Elvis performed his second concert at Long Beach Auditorium in

Elvis's daughter, Lisa Marie, cuts the ribbon at the opening of Presley Place, housing units for the homeless.

Long Beach, California. Four-year-old Lisa Marie was there that night:

> *My little daughter is in the audience. Lisa's here. I dedicate this show to her. She's right down there. This is the first time she's ever seen her daddy make a fool of himself in front of fourteen thousand people.*

On September 2, 1974, Elvis gave his closing show of a two-week engagement at the Las Vegas Hilton [formerly the International] in Las Vegas. He gave a terrific, longer performance, including a rare duet with Sherrill Nielson. Priscilla and Lisa Marie were in the audience as was Elvis's current girlfriend Sheila Ryan. Elvis, still shaken by his divorce, shared this with the audience:

> *[After singing You Gave Me a Mountain:] I want to make one thing clear. I've been singing that song for a long time. A lot of people kinda got it associated with me because*

> *they think it's a personal thing. But it's not. It's a beautiful song written by Marty Robbins. I heard Frankie Lane do it—I think it was—and I just love the song. It has nothing to do with me personally or my ex-wife Priscilla. She's right here. Honey, stand up. Turn around. Let them see you. Boy, she's beautiful, isn't she! I tell you for sure, damn. Show off my little daughter Lisa. She's six years old. Look at her jump up. Pull your dress down, Lisa. You pull your*

Priscilla Presley and Elvis at his Circle G Ranch in Mississippi in August 1968

*dress down before you jump up like that again, young lady.
And then at the same booth is my girlfriend Sheila [Ryan].
Stand up, Sheila. Turn around. Sheila, hold that ring up,
hold the ring up. The ring. Your right hand. Look at that
son of a bitch. No, the thing I'm trying to get across here is
we're the very best of friends and always have been. Our
divorce came about not because of another man or another
woman, but because of the circumstances involving my
career. I was traveling too much. I was gone too much, and
it was just an agreement that I didn't think it was fair to her
because I was gone so much and everything, so therefore as
decently as you can do that sort of thing, we just made an
agreement to always be friends and be close and care,
because we have a daughter to raise, and for her to have
whatever she wanted as a settlement. After the settlement
it came out about two million dollars. Well, after that I got
her a mink coat, XKE Jag after the settlement. Just gave it to
her. She got me—listen to this—tonight a $42,000 white
Rolls Royce. It's the type of relationship we have. [laughs]
It's not a bad set-up, is it fellows? You know, I mean I got
part of it back anyway, didn't I? I wasn't hurting too bad,
but I mean I did get part of it back. She bought the car just
out of a gesture of love and she liked this Stutz that I have.
A Stutz. She likes this stud [laughs]. Mike Stone [Priscilla's
boyfriend] ain't no stud. So forget it. She likes this Stutz,
and so I will give her the Stutz and she will give me the
Rolls. Stone better wish he was a stud. You know, he's a
[pause] nice guy.*

Elvis shared his feelings about his mother during a 1956 interview while on tour:

*My mother—she is always worried about a wreck, or
somethin' . . . me gettin' sick . . . so I have to let her know,
'cause she's not in real good health anyway. And if she*

worries too much it might not be good for her. So I make a habit of callin' every day or so.

Elvis talked about his father Vernon during a 1950s interview:

He's more help at home than he is anywhere else, because he can take care of all my business and he can look after things when I'm gone.

My father takes care of all my personal business. He's employed. I mean, he's just like on a salary, but he takes care of all the personal business, banking and any transactions, he handles it all.

During his June 9, 1972, New York press conference, Elvis mentioned his father Vernon:

Will I talk to my father? I have to [laughs], he handles all my personal affairs.

A reporter once asked Elvis if his parents worried about him while he's out on the road:

The only thing they worry about is wrecks and stuff like that. As far as getting in any kind of trouble, I know they don't worry about it. The only kind of trouble I ever been in is . . . I was stealin' eggs when I was real little [laughs].

During his last television special for CBS in 1977, Elvis introduced his father Vernon to the audience:

Ladies and gentlemen, I'd like to introduce you to my father. Uh, you know, he's been sick for a while but he's doing very well. Would you stand up with me, Daddy? Uh, he came here tonight. Come over here so they can see you . . . I really missed him because it's been a couple of years since he's been able to go on tour with me, you know. He's been sick.

At a late 1970s concert, Elvis talked about his father Vernon having a heart attack and how happy he was that he was better and on tour again:

> I'd like to tell you something if I could. Just one second, please. Just hang loose for a minute. Now recently, my father had a very serious, uh, heart attack, and he was very ill. But he's doing fantastic. I'm glad to see that. He's up and about and he's here tonight. Daddy! [applause]

In the midst of Elvis's last Las Vegas engagement, his father was put in the hospital. That night, Elvis was rushed getting ready for his show because he had to pick his father Vernon up from the hospital:

> You talk about getting ready fast. Lord have mercy. I drove my daddy back, out of the hospital today and he's fine.

During an interview in 1962, Elvis explained why he hired his cousin Billy Smith to work for him:

> Billy, who's my cousin—he's a little guy, and he had to quit school early. He had to quit school early to get a job, and he had a hard time finding a job because of his size, so I gave him a job, and he . . . his name is Billy Smith. And he's one of my mother's relatives. He does little jobs.

Hy Gardner asked Elvis in the midst of his 1950s controversy if he thought of himself as being well-behaved:

> Yes. I was raised in a pretty decent home and everything. My folks always made me behave whether I wanted to or not.

When asked about his parent's response to his success, Elvis answered:

> They're very thankful for it. I mean we always led a kind of a common life. We never had any luxuries, but we were

never real hungry . . . I guess they're just real proud, just like I am.

The small "shotgun house" where Elvis was born in Tupelo

Elvis talked about his mother Gladys learning to swim:

And mama, my best girl, is learning how to swim.

Elvis was once asked by Canadian disc jockey Red Robinson how his career affected his parents:

In a lot of different ways. They're just like they've always been, I mean as far as being themselves. But it's kind of a strain on them because, you know, people never leave them alone; I mean to be truthful about it.

On September 22, 1958, before sailing to Germany, Elvis spoke of the recent death of his mother:

I suppose since I was an only child that we might've been a little closer than . . . I mean, everyone loves their mother, but I was an only child, and Mother was always right with me all my life. And it wasn't only like losing a friend, a companion, someone to talk to. I could wake her up any hour of the night, and if I was worried or troubled by something, well, she'd get up and try to help me. I used to get very angry at—when I was growing up. It's a natural thing

when a young person wants to go somewhere or do some-
thing and your mother won't let you, you think, "Why,
what's wrong with you?" But then later on in the years you
find out, you know, that she was right. That she was only
doing it to protect you, to keep you from getting in any trou-
ble or getting hurt. And I'm very happy that she was kinda
strict on me, very happy that it worked out the way it did.

Elvis discussed the tragedy of losing his mother:

Such as like losing my mother while I was in the army, and
although I think that things like that, as tragic as they are,
tend to make you a better human being, really, 'cause you,
you can learn more about yourself. It gives you a better
understanding of yourself as well as other people. And it
can only help.

On July 3, 1960, Elvis's father Vernon married Davada "Dee"
Elliot Stanley in Huntsville, Alabama. Dee had three children:
Billy, Ricky, and David. Elvis did not attend the wedding. He
became very fond of his little stepbrothers. During his August
11, 1973, midnight show Elvis dedicated the song *The First
Time Ever I Saw Your Face* to his stepmother:

I'd like to do this next song for my stepmother. She's sitting
in a booth with my father right there. Stand up Dee. The
First Time Ever I Saw Your Face.

On March 17, 1974, Elvis played Mid-South Coliseum in his
hometown Memphis, Tennessee. During the show, Elvis joked
with his stepbrother Rick Stanley:

What are you doing, Strangelove? [Elvis's nickname for
Stanley] Weirdo. My stepbrother Ricky, man. He's weird.

If I Can Dream

(Elvis on Success)

Elvis was a dreamer. He wanted to be an entertainer, and he would often daydream about what he wanted to accomplish in life. It worked for him:

> When I was a child, ladies and gentlemen, I was a dreamer. I read comic books and I was the hero of the comic book. I saw movies and I was the hero in the movie. So every dream that I ever dreamed has come true a hundred times.

Elvis used visualization to help reach his goals, as he stated on a 1956 fan magazine album insert titled *The Truth About Me*:

> Well, when I was drivin' a truck—every time a big shiny car drove by, it started me sort of daydreaming. I always felt that someday, somehow, something would happen to change everything for me. And I'd daydream about how it would be.

On September 19, 1956, Elvis was interviewed in San Antonio, Texas. He had recently made a controversial appearance on the *Ed Sullivan Show*, which had earned the highest ratings in television history. During the interview, Elvis was asked about his movie contract:

> It's a dream come true, you know. It's something I never thought would happen to me, of all people. It just shows

that you can never tell what's going to happen to you in life. It's with Paramount Pictures and a seven-year contract. I've had people ask me was I going to sing in the movies. I'm not. Not as far as I know, because I took strictly an acting test, and actually I wouldn't care too much about singing in the movies.

As it turned out, his manager Colonel Parker discouraged movies with non-singing roles the rest of his career. Elvis's movies would become star vehicles for Elvis, the singer, and Elvis never got to develop his acting ability to its full potential.

In the mid-1950s Elvis stated his thoughts on his popularity:

If you want to get ahead, you gotta be different.

During a press conference on September 22, 1958, Elvis was asked if his success was due to luck or unusual talent:

Well, sir, I've been very lucky. I've been very lucky, and I happened to come along at a time in the music business where there was no trend. I was lucky, I mean the people were looking for something different, and I was lucky. I came along just in time.

Elvis gave one of his last major press conferences on June 9, 1972, before his historic first appearance at Madison Square Garden in New York City. He was the first performer to sell out four shows in three days. Some eighty thousand fans saw him in action, and the shows grossed $730,000. Two albums resulted from his June 10 appearances. Elvis shared his thoughts on keys to success at the press conference. On being asked how he outlasted other performers, he replied:

I take vitamin E [laughs]. I was only kidding. I don't know, dear. I just—I enjoy the business. I like what I'm doing.

One of the keys to success is doing something you love. Elvis shared this fact with his fans during his College Park, Maryland, show on September 28, 1974:

> *You see, folks, I love what I do. I love show bidness, bidness, business. No. I do man. I dig it. See, a lot of people go out there and they breeze through it. "Well, I got to work tonight." Not me. Hot damn! I love it. I ain't kidding you.*

Elvis belting out in song in 1974

Elvis thought learning consideration for other people's feelings was one of the greatest lessons one could learn in life:

> *My biggest thing would be consideration for other people's feelings. Anything you can do to keep yourself from becoming hardened—therefore making you—I think a better human being.*

Elvis had a great business manager. Colonel Tom Parker approached Elvis, and they became partners. It was one of the greatest partnerships in entertainment history. If you can afford it, it pays to have the best managers:

> *I don't think I'd ever been very big if it wasn't for him [Colonel Parker]. He's a very smart man.*

On August 31, 1957, Elvis gave an interview in Vancouver, Canada, during the afternoon before his only concert out of the country:

> *Actually I wasn't known at all until Colonel Parker started managing me, you see, and I got on RCA Victor and on television. Then I started being known.*

Elvis believed nobody becomes a success without help:

> *The great backing that I've had—the people and my managers and my assistants and all that sort of stuff—have really done a wonderful job. Everybody's just been really, really helpin' me.*

~

> *If you don't have people backin' you, people pushin' you, well, you might as well quit.*

Elvis wasn't the most gifted speaker, but he was a great communicator. He always acknowledged people, from the janitors of the coliseums he played to the President of the United

States. Elvis always used a person's name to make him or her feel important:

> *It's been a pleasure seeing you again, Charlie, and all these wonderful people in San Antonio . . . thank you, Charlie (April 15, 1956, interview with Charlie Walker).*

Acknowledging and praising his fans was a top priority for Elvis, and it was something he reminded his employees to do. He once gave a rare Monday afternoon performance:

> *I cannot believe we did a show on a Monday afternoon. I don't know how these people got off from work, how they got out of school or what happened. But they were here. I don't know how anybody's here, but I tell you one thing. We're sure glad you're here, son.*

Elvis's business philosophy was that if what you're doing is working, don't change it. This proved true with his movie formula for musicals. They all were a financial success:

> *I'm still staying with the same pattern. [regarding his singing style in 1956]*

> *You can't go out of your capabilities—your limitations. You have to know your capabilities. If I can entertain people with what I am doing—well, I'd be a fool to tamper with it, to try to change it. You're better off if what you're doing is doing okay—you're better off stickin' with it until time itself changes things. I mean that's what I believe (1962 Jack Bentley interview).*

Elvis was a very hard worker, but he also knew the importance of having some down time:

> *I like to work, but I like to have a little time off, too—where I don't have to do anything.*

In 1956, an interviewer informed Elvis that he had probably sold more records for RCA than any other recording artist:

> *I don't know. I hate to say yeah—it'll sound like I'm bragging.*

Elvis's philosophy was that if people like what you are doing then you should go the extra mile for them. That's good business.

> *It just makes me want to knock myself out to keep giving 'em something they enjoy. I hope I can keep giving 'em stuff that they like.*

～

> *If they act like they're with you it makes you put more into it.*

Contributing to his longevity was the fact that Elvis hired the best musicians and the best sound equipment. During his September 28, 1974, show he shared his thoughts on this with the fifteen thousand fans in attendance:

> *We carry our own sound equipment. We carry the best equipment that money can buy. We have the most expensive show on the road, but I do not care. I want the people to get the best!*

During an interview in 1972, Elvis talked about his talented musicians and the inspiration he received from them:

> *What's interesting about . . . about music, and about all the people [his musicians] here. They find new sounds, and they do things differently themselves. So it's like a new experience every day. The guy on the guitar will find a new lick, or the guy on the piano will find something, or the voices will add something. And I hear all this and it inspires me. I like it.*

I've never gotten over what they call stage fright. I go through it every show. I'm pretty concerned. I'm pretty much thinking about the show. I never get completely comfortable with it, and I don't let the people with me get comfortable with it in that I remind them it's a new crowd out there. It's a new audience, and they haven't seen us before—so it's got to be like the first time we go on. I don't like to stay backstage too long, you know. I've got to please the crowd. I mean I've got to excite them or make them happy and gear myself to doing that show. And, uh, somebody will, uh, walk up to me and say, "Hey, your head just exploded." I won't hear it.

On January 14, 1973, Elvis made history by becoming the first entertainer to perform a live concert via satellite to forty countries. "Elvis: Aloha from Hawaii" was the highest rated show at the time. It was estimated that the viewing audience was more than one billion (a larger audience than viewed man's first walk on the moon). It was a benefit show for the Kui Lee Cancer Fund. It raised more than $75,000. Elvis was humbled by doing such a show:

Whew! It's very hard to comprehend it because I—in fifteen years, it's hard to comprehend that happening . . . out to all the countries all over the world via satellite, it's very difficult to comprehend . . . I like to get the rapport with an audience, 'cause it's a give and take thing. If you can do that, it works, you know. If the artist, or whoever is performing, can get that kind of rapport going with an audience, then it really pays off. It's good, you know. A live concert to me is exciting because of all the electricity that's generated in the crowd and on stage, but it's my favorite part of show, of the business, is the live concert.

I'd just like to say before anything else, uh—that it's a great privilege, uh, to do this satellite program, and I'm going to do my best and all the people that work with me, to do a good show. Which is just pure entertainment. No messages, no this, no that.

Regarding his incredible overnight success:

I've had some very lucky and wonderful breaks.

Elvis's motto was "Taking Care of Business." He designed a necklace featuring the letters TCB over a lightning bolt. That symbol meant to Take Care of Business in a flash. Elvis gave these necklaces to his employees and close friends. He had a special ring designed for himself that featured the emblem:

Let me explain something to you. A lot of people ask me about this ring [TCB]. I don't know what it is. Naw, really. It has, you know, the diamonds, the TCB—which is Taking Care of Business, and the lightning bolt. My birth stone is the black diamond. Swear to God. I have never in my life heard of a black diamond, much less seen one. So, it took me fourteen years. I got it from a collector in Denver, Colorado. It doesn't shine. It doesn't do anything. It's just a black diamond.

An original TCB necklace. It stood for Elvis's motto "Takin' Care of Business." Elvis would give these to his employees and friends.

Mr. Songman

(Elvis on Show Business)

Elvis on Tour was Elvis Presley's thirty-third and last film. It was a documentary of his fifteen-city tour in April, 1972. It was voted best documentary of that year by the Hollywood Foreign Press Association. The producers interviewed Elvis to use his voice as a narrative throughout the film:

> My daddy had seen a lot of people who, uh, played the guitar and stuff, who didn't work. So, he said, "You should make up your mind," he said, "about either being an electrician or playing the guitar." He said, "I never saw a guitar player that was worth a damn" [laughs].

In a 1950s interview, Elvis discussed his first guitar:

> My first guitar cost me $12.95, when I was thirteen. When I bought a new one, the man gave me eight dollars on the trade-in, then threw it in the wastebasket. Shucks, it still played good!

Elvis comments on singing material:

> Your material can make you or break you. If you sing a good song, naturally it will sell. If you sing a bad one . . .

Elvis spoke about the music industry during his 1968 NBC-TV special:

I'd like to talk a little bit about music. Very little. [laughs] There's been a big change in the music field in the last ten or twelve years. I think everything has improved. The sounds have improved, the musicians have improved, the engineers have certainly improved. I like a lot of the new groups, you know. The Beatles and the Byrds and whoever. But I really like a lot of the new music—a lot of it is basically—our music is basically—rock 'n' roll—is basically gospel or rhythm and blues, or it sprang from that. People have been adding to it, adding instruments to it, experimenting with it.

During Elvis's February 27, 1970, Houston Astrodome press conference, he talked about his concept of music:

See, country music was always a part of the influence on my type of music, anyway—a combination of country music, gospel, rhythm and blues all combined is what it really was.

Elvis in Fort Worth, Texas, in 1972

In another 1956 interview, Elvis was asked what would happen if he stopped wiggling on stage:

Well, sir, if you take the wiggle out of it [rock 'n' roll], it's finished.

On March 24, 1956, Elvis was interviewed by Robert Carton. He was asked about the flashy clothes he wears:

On the streets—out in public—I like real conservative clothes. Somethin' that's not too flashy. But on stage I like 'em as flashy as you can get 'em. On stage your clothes play a very important part in it.

Elvis joked with a Las Vegas audience in August of 1969:

Every time I put this thing [his guitar] on I feel like I got a machine gun, man, you know [Drummer makes machine gun sound on drums].

At a later date in Las Vegas, Elvis talked with his fans about his ability to play the guitar:

Contrary to a lot of people's belief I can play this thing [his guitar] a little bit.

During another Las Vegas show in 1969 Elvis introduced his lead guitar player, James Burton. Presley phoned Burton earlier that year to ask that he put together a band for his upcoming Las Vegas engagement. Burton, the leader of Elvis's band, had written the music and played on the Dale Hawkins hit *Suzy Q*, and he also had played lead guitar for singer Ricky Nelson:

Young man on lead guitar—he's one of the finest guitar players I've ever met. His name is James Burton, ladies and gentlemen. James.

Elvis and lead guitarist James Burton in concert

Elvis liked to play on words:

> *[Introducing his band] Sounds like* Dating Game, *man.*
> *And so and so and so and so, you know. Young man on*
> *drums—he hails from Dallas, Texas. Big "D." His name is*
> *Ronnie Tutt, ladies and gentlemen. Ronnie Tutt. Young*
> *man on bass—his name is Jerry Scheff. Jerry. So his name is*
> *Tutt. His name is Scheff. It's Tutt. Scheff, anyway you look*
> *at it, man [laughs].*

Elvis joked with his fans during a 1970s Las Vegas engagement:

> *We've got so many songs. I'd like to explain—so many*
> *songs that I have recorded and done in movies and—there*
> *are so many things that I've done that . . . not recorded*
> *that I don't want you to know nothing about, you know.*
> *[laughter] I have to occasionally turn around and ask what*
> *I'm doing next because we've got so many songs. Big*
> *deal, you know.*

Elvis performed so many high-energy songs that he would have to take a break to catch his breath. It was during these times that Elvis loved to tease his audience:

> *You know, leaning up against this piano drinking water, it's about as nice as you can get. About as casual as you can get. It's lazy, is what it is, I tell ya.*

On November 10, 1971, during a concert in Boston, Massachusetts, Elvis joked with members of his orchestra:

> *[Introducing members of his orchestra] The Tony Bruno Orchestra, ladies and gentlemen. That's the entire northeast members of the Mafia. You guys all Mafia! Tony Bruno. Don't kid me with that name, man.*

In a Nashville recording session on January 17, 1968, Elvis revealed his human side and the fact that he didn't record songs perfectly on the first take. He expressed dissatisfaction with a particular take by exclaiming:

> *That ain't worth a shit!*

On returning to live performing again in the late sixties, Elvis hired the best singers and musicians he could find. He often shared his stage with them.

> *I'd like you to say hello to J. D. Sumner and the Stamps Quartet. This man [J. D.] is the world's lowest bass singer—in more ways than one.*

> *On the piano from Lubbock, Texas, is Glen Campbell, naw, Glenn Hardin.*

Elvis gave his drummer a special introduction to his own home crowd:

On the drums from Dallas, Texas, is Ronnie Tutt [plays drum solo]. Yeah! Ronnie. Stand up, son. Stand up. Stand up, Ronnie. You've been sitting down long enough. Fantastic.

~

The fellow that gives me my water and my scarves and sings harmony with me. He's my friend, Charlie Hodge.

~

First of all, on the left, Mr. J. D. Sumner and the Stamps Quartet. I've told the story before, I'm gonna tell it again. When I was sixteen years old I was listening to him sing bass with a group called the Blackwood Brothers, in Memphis, Tennessee. And I never dreamed I'd be singing with him on stage. It's a pleasure, J. D.

~

He [J. D. Sumner] can do better than that, ladies and gentlemen. He's the world's lowest bass singer, and that was too easy, J. D. That was really too easy for you. I mean, you hold the record of being the lowest human being in the—I mean the lowest bass singer.

~

James [Burton] can play the guitar on the back of his head, you know—better than John [Wilkinson] can in front. Naw, I'm only kidding, John. Only kidding.

~

Talking about his song *It's Now or Never*, which was taken from the Italian song *O Sole Mio*:

I'm going to ask Sherrill, the weird kid with the sunglasses on, I'm going to ask him to sing the . . . is it E or I! [pronunciation] What is it! E-talian version—okay. I said that one time to a reporter, just talking. He printed it e-y-e.

Elvis sang the song *My Way* throughout the 1970s:

That's a very good song, ladies and gentlemen, but I wouldn't want it associated with my own personal life. "Now the end is near" and all that jazz. It's a nice song. It's okay for Sinatra. I haven't even ate it up and spit it out yet—I'm still chewing on it. Naw, it's a good song.

During one monologue in Las Vegas in the summer of 1969, Elvis talked about his early days as a musician:

When I started out, I had three pieces. [laughs] I mean, instruments. I had a guitar, a shaky leg, another guitar, and another shaky leg. So, we did about five songs before anyone knew who we were.

When I first started out, I was a child.

Elvis remembered his very first live appearance during an interview on August 6, 1956:

My very first appearance after I started recording, I was on a show in Memphis where I started doing that [stage movements]. I was on the show as an extra added single. A big jamboree in an outdoor theatre—outdoor auditorium—and I came out on stage and I was scared stiff. It was my first big appearance in front of an audience. I came out, and I was doing a fast-type tune. One of my first records and, uh, everybody was hollering, and I didn't know what they were hollering at. Everybody was screaming and everything. I came off stage, and my manager told me they was hollering because I was wiggling my legs, and I was unaware of what I was doing. So I went back out for an encore and I did a little more. The more I did, the louder it went.

During his February 27, 1970, press conference in Houston, Texas, Elvis discussed his first shows:

To tell you the truth, I started out here in Texas. I think the first shows that I worked was down here around Houston, and all over Texas.

Though Elvis was born in Tupelo, Mississippi, he always referred to his hometown as being Memphis, Tennessee. Elvis often remarked about playing his hometown:

I don't work it very often, because I don't think it's very good to work your home town very much. (1956 interview)

On March 20, 1974, Elvis played to an enthusiastic hometown audience:

It's always been said that a person cannot return to their hometowns, but you have disproven that theory completely. You have really made it worthwhile.

Elvis's favorite music was gospel. He received three Grammy awards, and all three were for his gospel performances. All through his career, Elvis sang his favorite gospel songs to his fans. Few singers would sing gospel in Las Vegas:

There's something I want to do before I leave here, because we've never done this before, and I've always had a hankering—hankering! Good grief. If you don't mind—and I know you've been sitting here for a long time. I'd like to do a couple a three spiritual songs for you, you know. I'm going to ask the Stamps to come out here and, uh, I don't know how you're going to do it, fellows—no, no. This is

MR. SONGMAN
(Elvis on Show Business)

*something new. I've never done this before. [Man yells,
"You're the king."] Thank you, sir. Fixing to sing about
Him. [Audience applauds.]*

Elvis's favorite gospel song was *How Great Thou Art*. He often
performed this song for his audiences as he did the evening of
November 11, 1970, in Portland, Oregon:

> *About four years ago, ladies and gentlemen, I did a gospel
> album. I won a Grammy for it—one of the songs in it.
> Called How Great Thou Art.*

In March of 1972, Elvis discussed his love for gospel music:

> *We grew up with it. From the time I was . . . I can remem-
> ber, like two years old, I grew up with this, because my
> folks took me there. When I got old enough, I started sing-
> ing in church. But I liked all types of music, you know.
> When I was in high school, I had records by Mario Lanza
> . . . and the Metropolitan Opera. I just, I loved music. The
> Spanish—I liked the Mexican flavored songs. But this
> thing here—the gospel thing—is just . . . gospel is really
> what we grew up with, more than anything else. We do
> two shows a lot of times. And we will go upstairs and sing
> until daylight, you know, gospel songs . . . I think it more or
> less puts your mind at ease. It does mine.*

Elvis sings to his fans.

You're The Devil in Disguise

(Elvis on Criticism)

Because of Elvis's suggestive movements on stage, his music, and outrageous clothing, parents, preachers, and the media made him a scapegoat for the nation's ills, in particular juvenile delinquency. Elvis, sensitive man that he was, was bothered by the public's reaction and made his feelings clear in numerous interviews in the 1950s:

> I don't see how they could think that it would contribute to juvenile delinquency. It's only singing and dancing. I don't see that, because if there's anything I've tried to do, I've tried to live a straight, clean life, and not set any kind of bad example. I will say there are people that are going to like you and people that don't like you regardless of what business you are in or what you do. You cannot please everyone.

Elvis made the following statement on a Hy Gardner television interview on July 1, 1956, in response to the negative press he had been receiving:

> I don't see that any type of music would have any bad influence on people, when it's only music. I can't figure it out. I mean in a lot of the papers, they say that rock 'n' roll is a big influence on juvenile delinquency. I don't think that it is. I don't feel that I am doing anything wrong.

Elvis was reminded that rock 'n' roll was outlawed in a northern California city in July of 1956 because people thought it led to juvenile delinquency:

> *I do not agree. Not only because I do it, but because it's untrue. Rock 'n' roll is a music. Why should a music contribute to rock 'n' roll, I mean contribute to juvenile delinquency! If people are gonna be juvenile delinquents, they're gonna be delinquents if they hear Mother Goose rhymes.*

Although he appreciated his audiences, Elvis had little tolerance for hecklers, as demonstrated during his August 30, 1974, Las Vegas 3:00 AM show:

> *[Girl yells, "I love you, Elvis!"] I love you too, sweetheart. Well, I don't take that for granted. [A man yells, "I hate you, Elvis!"] Fuck you! [audience cheers]*

In the summer of 1956, Elvis, who was often billed as the nation's only atomic-powered singer, found himself in a whirlwind of controversy over his dance moves. A Miami, Florida, journalist wrote that Elvis was "the biggest freak in modern show business history" and a "no-talent performer." He also called him an "idiot's delight" and referred to the kids who attended his shows as "a bunch of idiots." Interviewed on August 6, Elvis responded in kind:

> *He ain't nothing but an idiot or he wouldn't sit up and write all that stuff. He just hates to admit that he's too old to have any more fun, you know. You have to put on a show for people. In other words, people can buy your records and hear you sing. They don't have to come out to hear you sing. You have to put on a show to draw a crowd. If I just stood out there and sang and never moved a muscle, people would say, "My goodness, I can stay home and listen to his records." You have to give them a show, something to talk about.*

During this same period, Elvis made the following statement in response to the bad press he had been receiving:

Those people [critics] have a job to do and they do it.

You gotta accept the bad along with the good. I've been getting some very good publicity. The press has been real wonderful to me. I have been given some bad publicity, but you have to accept that, and I know I'm doin' the best I can. I've never turned a disc jockey down, because they're the people that help make you in this business.

During an Ottawa, Canada, interview on April 3, 1957, Elvis again responded to the controversy over his singing style:

There's gonna be people that don't like ya. There were people that didn't like Jesus Christ. They killed him, and Jesus Christ was a perfect man. And there's gonna be people that don't like you regardless of who you are or what you do, because if everybody thought the same way, they'd be drivin' the same car, everybody'd be marryin' the same woman and that wouldn't work out [laughs].

Well, I tell ya, in a place where I feel that I'm gonna have to do my best, I'm not as much at ease as I am at a place where I know there's no critics.

During a 1957 March of Dimes Galaxy of Stars interview, Elvis again elaborates on the criticism he had been receiving for his stage performances:

Some people have the idea I'm a controversial influence on the young folks. Whatever I do, I always want to do my best for teenagers. I certainly never wanna do anything that would be a wrong influence. When I sing, I just—I just sing from my heart . . . As long as I live, I'll never stop being grateful to the American people for giving me this big break.

At his College Park, Maryland, concert on September 28, 1974, Elvis was upset because a journalist had commented on his midriff:

I'd like to say something right here. Those of you who saw the morning paper, evening paper, whatever it was—they gave us a fantastic write-up. Now they did, except they said I had a paunch here. I want to tell you something. I got their damn paunch. I wore a bulletproof vest on stage. True. In case some fool decides to take a twenty-two and blow my belly button off. That's the truth. I got his [journalist] paunch. Son of a bitch.

I'd like to pass on a bit of information for ya—to ya. Things that are written in movie magazines about me are trash! Rumors that you hear about me are trash! I'm an 8th degree black belt in karate. I am a federal narcotics agent. I am. Swear to God. No, you can do whatever you want to do, I'm just sayin' that I am. They don't give you that if you're strung out—if you done this. No, no, no, no, no, no. On the contrary, I have to be straight as an arrow because I'm around people all the time. I don't like to get out of it in either way. I don't drink booze. I don't take any of this 'n that. [Applause] No, no, now wait a minute. [Someone calls, "Boo."] By God, don't say "boo," son. I'll whip your ass. I mean, don't say "boo" to me when I tell you that, because I'm tellin' you the God's truth. And that's not to cover anything. It's just to tell you the truth about the matter. You can take my word or you can take the goddamn movie magazines, you know. [applause] [On December 21, 1970, Elvis met with President Richard Nixon at the

White House. Nixon presented Elvis with a federal nar-cotics bureau badge. Elvis asked the president if he could invite into the oval office his two friends Jerry Schilling and Sonny West. Nixon complied.]

During a 1970s concert Elvis quips about the wiggling he did back in the 1950s:

My Fruit of the Looms were too tight.

From July 31 through August 28, 1969, Elvis performed at the International Hotel in Las Vegas—his first concerts before a live audience in more than eight years. In the middle of each performance, he would pull up a stool and talk about his child-hood, how he had gotten into the business, his experiences in the army, his movie career, and how he had started missing direct contact with audiences. Audiences hung on every word:

You think sideburns are weird now. Back in the fifties, man, people would yell, "Get him, get him, he's a squirrel." People wondered why I shook so much.

Elvis rockin' in 1974

Soldier Boy

(Elvis on the Army)

Elvis was drafted into the U.S. Army on December 19, 1957. He was inducted on March 24, 1958. Presley was assigned serial number 53310761 and did his basic training at Fort Hood, Texas. Elvis requested no special treatment. On September 22, 1958, Elvis boarded the USS *General Randall* for Bremerhaven, West Germany, where he served out the remainder of his time. He was discharged as a buck sergeant on March 5, 1960:

> *I, Elvis Presley, do solemnly swear that I will bear true faith and allegiance to the United States of America.*

During a press conference on September 22, 1958, in Brooklyn, New York, Elvis was asked about his military medals:

> *These medals right here, ma'am, are for expert with a carbine rifle and also tank weapons. Tank weapon. That's a ninety-millimeter gun. And this one right here, I didn't do quite as well. It's the pistol.*

Elvis was asked about rock 'n' roll and the criticism he had received before he was drafted:

> *Sir, the wiggle can't straighten out. [laughs] If you do, you're finished. It's like the guy down in Fort Hood . . . one of the sergeants one day . . . I was . . . I was sitting down on my foot locker, and my left leg was shaking. I*

*mean just unconsciously. He said, "Presley, I wish you'd
quit shaking that leg." I said, "Sarge, when that leg quits
shaking I'm finished."*

Elvis was asked if he was going to take advantage of any educational benefits while in the armed services:

*Well, I have thought a lot about the different types of
schooling the army has to offer. And I do know for a fact
that a lot of fellows have gone through the service and
benefited out in civilian life, after they came out of the service. A lot of guys that had nothing prior to the time they
went in, and they go in service and they take some kind of a
schooling for maybe a year or two years, and when they
come out of the army, well, they're qualified for a good job.
Now, it doesn't hurt for anybody to have a profession to
turn to in case something did happen to the entertainment
business, or something happen to me. I don't know exactly
yet what kind of school that I would like to go to.*

Following that, Elvis was asked if the boys had given him a rough time because he was famous:

*No sir, I was very surprised. I've never met a better group
of boys in my life. They probably would have if it'd been
like everybody thought. I mean, everybody thought I
wouldn't have to work, that I would be given special
treatment and this and that. But when they looked around
and saw I was on KP and I was pulling guard and everything just like they were, well, they figured, "Well, he's
just like us."*

On October 1, 1958, Elvis arrived at Bremerhaven, West Germany, aboard the USS *General Randall.* Some eleven hundred European fans greeted him. The next day, Elvis was interviewed at the Enlisted Men's Club at the Thirty-Second Armored Battalion in Friedberg, Germany:

I would just like to say, ladies and gentlemen, that it's really a privilege to be in Europe. It's something that I have looked forward to for some time. I consider it a privilege to be assigned to such a fine outfit as the Third Armored Division. I hope that I can live up to everybody's expectations of me, and I will do my very best to. I only regret that I can't do some shows and different things while I am here, but I will be looking forward to when my army hitch is over. I would like very much to come back on a regular tour.

Elvis never did return to Europe to tour. One reason was that the Dutch-born Colonel Parker, worried that his status as an illegal alien might be discovered, talked Elvis out of playing in any foreign countries besides Canada. Another concern was the amount of security that would be involved in a world tour.

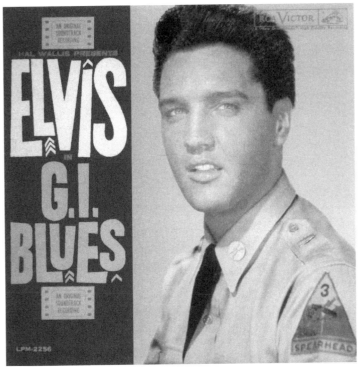

Elvis's first movie after his discharge from the army was *G. I. Blues*.

In 1958, while stationed in Germany, Elvis gave a brief interview to a German journalist who wondered why he wasn't performing there:

> *I was sent over here by the army to be a soldier. Understand? And it would not be fair to the other boys in the army if I were traveling around and singing. I cannot be treated any different from the other boys. Do you understand? I am very sorry that I am not here as an entertainer—as a singer, but maybe, I hope, when I'm out of the army, someday I can come back to Europe on a tour and then I will travel around as an entertainer.*

On August 23, 1969, during his Las Vegas dinner show, Elvis shared some of his army experiences with his audience:

> *I got drafted and overnight it was all gone. It was like a dream. I was—like, was that me? Did it really happen? So all the guys in the service just watched me to see what was going to happen. I'd try to play the rifle, you know. They watched me to see what I was going to do, and when they saw it was the same as them, everything was okay. But the guys in the service must get awfully homesick because they call each other mother a lot. [laughter]*

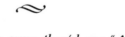

> *When I was in the army they'd say "Attention." I'm going. They'd say, "Watch him. He's a squirrel boy. Right out of the trees."*

On March 3, 1960, Elvis arrived at McGuire Air Force Base in New Jersey, following his discharge. He later went to Fort Dix for a press conference where a reporter asked him if his sobering army life had changed his mind about rock 'n' roll.

*Sobering army life? No, it hasn't changed my mind,
because I was in tanks for a long time, and they rock and
roll quite a bit.*

Elvis reflects on his army experience during a press conference
in 1960:

*It's been a big help in both my career and my personal life,
because I learned a lot. I made a lot friends that I never
would have met otherwise and I've had a lot of good experiences . . . and some bad ones, naturally. It's good to rough
it—to put yourself to a test. To see if you can take it. To see
if you can stand it.*

Elvis's thoughts on others going into the service:

*The only thing I can say is to play it straight and do your
best, because you can't fight 'em. [laughs] They never lost
yet. [laughs] And you can't fight 'em. So, you can make it
easy or you can make it hard on yourself. I mean, if you
play it straight and get the people on your side—let 'em
know you're trying. You, as the army would say, you've
got it made. And if you're going to try to be an individual
or try to be different—you're gonna go through two years
of . . . misery. [laughs]*

Elvis jokes about his army days during a Las Vegas performance in 1969:

*The guys in the army must get very homesick . . . 'cause
they call each other "mother." I picked it up, but you know
that was only the half of it. [laughs] It didn't go over so
good when I got back to Hollywood. Director would say
"Hello, Mr. Presley," I'd say "Hello there, mother . . ."*

During his June 9, 1972, press conference Elvis was asked his
opinion of war protesters:

Honey, I'd just soon to keep my own personal views about that to myself. 'Cause I'm just an entertainer and I'd rather not say.

Graceland Mansion, Elvis's home for the last twenty years of his life

Memories

(Elvis on Movies)

Elvis Presley loved movies. The first film he ever saw was *Abbott and Costello Meet Frankenstein*. As a teenager, he worked at a movie theater so he could see movies for free. On April 1, 1956, Elvis performed a screen test for producer Hal Wallis. He sang *Blue Suede Shoes* and performed a scene from *The Rainmaker*. Wallis was impressed with Presley, and five days later, Elvis signed a seven-year contract with Paramount Pictures. It was something Elvis had dreamed about:

> *It's a dream come true, you know. It's something I never thought would happen to me of all people.*

In a later interview, Elvis mentions his desire to be an actor:

> *All of my life, I've wanted to be an actor, though I never was in any school plays or recited a line other than the "Gettysburg Address" for my sixth-grade homeroom class. But always sticking in the back of my head was the idea that somehow, someday, I'd like to get the chance to act.*

> *I'll tell you something about Hollywood. It's a great place. At least, I've had the kicks there. I just finished my first movie for Twentieth Century Fox, called* Love Me Tender, *and you know, it was the biggest thrill of my life. Making pictures is, well, I don't know exactly what to call it, except*

that it's different. It's something I've always wanted to do. And I just hope you'll like me on the screen because I'd sure like to keep on making pictures for you.

Elvis discusses his recent movie contract in late August of 1956:

There have been a lot of articles come out that I was gonna imitate or copy the late James Dean, or something like that, but I've never thought about it, although James Dean was one of the greatest actors I've ever seen. He and Marlon Brando, and a whole bunch more I could recall. But I'm not going to try to copy anybody. In fact, I don't even know if I can act or not. I'm just gonna give it a try.

In August 1959, in Bad Nauheim, Germany, Elvis conducted a telephone interview with Dick Clark, who asked him about his plans for his movie career after he got out of the army:

And then I have three pictures to make; one for Mr. Wallis and then the other two for Twentieth Century Fox.

On August 31, 1957, Elvis was interviewed by Canadian disc jockey Red Robinson, who asked him about his career in film:

I think it's great. In fact, I like it better than any phase of the business other than the public appearances. I like movies better than I do TV work. If you goof in the movies, you can go back and take it over. In TV, you just goof.

Robinson asked Elvis about acting:

There is nobody that helps you out. They have a director and a producer. As far as the acting and as far as the singing and all—you're on your own. I mean nobody tells you how to do that. You have to learn it yourself. That's something you learn through experience. I think that maybe I might accomplish something at it through the years. When you start trying to act, you're dead.

On March 8, 1960, after returning home from the army Elvis held a press conference. He was asked about his upcoming movies:

> I have three pictures in a row to do. I hope they won't be rock 'n' roll pictures 'cause I have made four already, and you can only get away with that for so long. I'm thinking in terms of, I'd like to do a little more of a serious role. Because my ambition is to progress as an actor, which takes a long time and a lot of experience. Well, it wouldn't hurt me any to go to school, but I learn best by experience. I never was very good in school is the thing. [laughs] And it's gonna take me a long time, and a lot of experience.

Elvis also talked about the shape of his movie career during a Las Vegas dinner show on August 23, 1969:

> So I went to Hollywood, and I wasn't ready for that town and they weren't ready for me, you know. First of all, you get a hit record. Then you go on television and then you go to Hollywood. That's how it happens. So I was out there. It was all new to me. I was like nineteen or twenty years old. It's all exciting and everybody was saying, "Hey, Mr. Presley, Mr. Presley, Mr. Presley!" Son of a bitch, you know [laughs]. I did Love Me Tender, Loving You, Loving Her, Loving Anybody I Could Get My Hands on at the Time [laughs]. I did Jailhouse Crock-Rock and I did King Creole. So I'd done four pictures and I was living it up. I was getting used to the movie star bit. You know, I had dark glasses on—you know, sitting in the back of a Cadillac limousine—saying I'm a movie star, I'm somebody, hey—eating hamburgers and drinking Pepsi-Colas. I was living it up, man.

During a 1956 interview, Elvis discussed his future movie career:

> I've had people ask me was I going to sing in the movies. I'm not. Not as far as I know, because I took strictly an

Montage of photos from a 1974, Fort Worth, Texas concert

acting test and actually I wouldn't care too much about singing in the movies.

In 1962, during a Jack Bentley Hollywood interview Elvis discussed his movie career. He had just completed his film *Girls, Girls, Girls*:

Like I have people say to me all the time, "Why don't you do an artistic picture!" I'd like to. I'd like to do something someday where I feel that I've done a good job as an actor in a certain type role. But I feel that it comes with time. In the meantime, if I can entertain people with the things I'm doing—well, I'd be a fool to tamper with it.

Elvis jokes about his movie career with his fans during his August 15, 1969, Las Vegas show:

After G.I. Blues and Blue Hawaii, I wrote an eight-millimeter picture called Up Your Nose. But it's not out yet. It's about a homesick little squirrel in the winter trying to find his nuts.

Elvis was respectful of other entertainers. He appreciated people with great talent as he expressed during a 1956 interview when he was compared to actor James Dean:

I would never compare myself in any way to James Dean, because James Dean was a genius in acting.

During a press conference in Houston, Texas, on February 27, 1970, Elvis was asked if he was going to keep making films:

I hope to [laughs] . . . Well, I'd like to make better films . . . well, better than the ones I made before.

On January 26, 1971, Elvis was performing at the International Hotel in Las Vegas. Producer Hal Wallis was in the audience:

My first big movie contract was with a gentlemen who's made about ten of my movies, and one we did, Blue Hawaii, has a song in it [Can't Help Falling in Love]; we usually close our show with it, but we're gonna do it early. I'd like to dedicate it to Mr. Wallis because he still makes very good films: Anne of a Thousand Days, True Grit. I'd like to dedicate this to you, Mr. Wallis.

During his August 12, 1971, Las Vegas show Elvis introduced actor Richard Egan:

My very first movie, ladies and gentlemen, was Love Me Tender, and I had the privilege of working with a very fine actor—he played my older brother—and we became very good friends since making that film. His name is Richard Egan. He's here tonight. Richard. I got killed in Love Me Tender; he [Egan] got the girl.

On May 9, 1976, at the Sahara Hotel, Nevada, Elvis discussed a movie scene he did with Joan Blackman, his costar in *Blue Hawaii*:

Did you see the movie Blue Hawaii? There's a funny thing that happened. My costar is Joan Blackman, and she had on the short-sleeve purple dress and white lei of flowers. I was dressed in white and had a red wrap. Anyway, we were moving down this moat, and people were throwing flowers, and people were singing the Hawaiian Wedding Song. The first time we did it, see, they had guys underneath the water pulling a cable, and the first time we did it they hit the side of the bank too hard, and the boat crashed right into it. Pow! It took me three hours to get remade-up and get ready to do it again. So we got married twice in the same day. Or did we? One other time in Viva Las Vegas with Ann-Margret, we got married. It took us a week to film that wedding scene. It is so real until you think you're married. It took us two years to figure out we weren't.

Let's Be Friends
(Elvis on Friendship)

Elvis Presley was a phenomenon not only to the general public, but also to celebrities. During his movie and Las Vegas years, countless stars came to see him. During his first Las Vegas run, fellow celebrities came to check out his act. Elvis always acknowledged them, including at his closing show on May 6, 1956:

> *I would like to dedicate my whole part of the show—and I hope they like something we do up here, even if it's wrong—to two celebrities that we have in the house. We may have more, but these two fellows I know are here. I'd like to do this little song here for them. Mr. Ray Bolger. He's in the audience. Mr. Ray Bolger and also for Mr. Phil Silvers. He's in the audience. Roy Acuff, he's out here somewhere.*

Bob Hope attended Elvis's August 20, 1973, midnight show at the Las Vegas Hilton [formerly the International]. Elvis said:

> *There's a gentleman in the audience I'd like you to meet, ladies and gentlemen. It's an honor for him to come and see our show. He's really an American institution. He's one of the funniest men that ever lived. Mr. Bob Hope. Thank you, sir. Thank you very much for coming in. It's been an honor. I'd like to do a gospel song, ladies and*

gentlemen. I dedicate this to Mr. Bob Hope. [Elvis sang How Great Thou Art.]

During Elvis's historic "Aloha from Hawaii" show, on January 14, 1973—the first satellite broadcast ever for an entertainer and viewed by an estimated one billion people worldwide—Elvis introduced his friend, actor Jack Lord, to the audience.

One of my favorite actors is in the audience. Jack Lord. I got to say that, you know. Hawaii Five-O, man.

Elvis introduced comedian/actor Bill Cosby during his September 2, 1974, closing show at the Las Vegas Hilton. Elvis got sick and missed a couple of shows during this engagement, and Cosby filled in for him:

When I got sick, a fellow volunteered his services to come in and fill in for me. He was way up north somewhere working or doing a TV show. He does so much. He volunteered to come in and work this show for me, and he's been here ever since. He'll open for me tomorrow night. I'd like to thank him. Bill Cosby. Bill, where are you buddy? Where's Bill? I haven't seen Bill yet. Where's Cosby? You mean after that buildup, the son of a bitch left. Well, to hell with him. I won't pay him anyway. Naw, I'm only kidding. No, he gets ten grand. I give him that whether he likes it or not. And stick it up his nose.

Actor Telly Savalas was in the audience at the opening show in Las Vegas on August 19, 1974:

There is someone else in the audience I want you to meet. He's one of the coolest actors in the world. He's been a friend of mine for a long, long time. He came on the movie set when I was doing a movie called Kid Galahad. *It was the first time I met him. He's been in to see my show and he's got the number-one show on television. Mr. Telly*

Savalas. Yes, sir. Nice to see you. "Thank you, Sweet-heart!" [a line from Kojak] [laughs]

Elvis shared these thoughts about other performers with interviewer Robert Carlton Brown on March 24, 1956:

In other words, I admire anybody that's good, regardless of what kind of singer they are. Whether they're religious, rhythm and blues, hillbilly, or anything else. If they're great, I mean I like 'em. From Roy Acuff on up to Mario Lanza. I just admire them if they're really great.

Elvis disclosed the type of friends he liked being around:

I don't want anybody that is more or less a snob or put-on. I'd want somebody to just be themselves.

You got so many friends. You got so many people you can go to if you need help.

Elvis frequently complimented other entertainers:

I wish I was like some of my rivals: Carl Perkins and Gene Vincent. Those guys—they're pretty good songwriters. But me, I did good to get out of high school.

Elvis frequently introduced his friends during his concerts:

In fact, his [Vernon Presley's] doctor's here tonight—Dr. Nick. Stand up, Dr. Nick. It's time, you know. I want you to watch something. There he is right there. See, the little gray-headed guy. He looks like a shorter version of my daddy, you know.

Elvis once wrote his philosophy for a happy life for his friend Pat Perry:

Elvis singing from the heart

"Philosophy For Happy Life"
Someone to love
Something to look
Forward to, and
Something to do

Elvis was always one to help the underdog. A Las Vegas Hilton Hotel restaurant employee that he befriended was in danger of losing his job, and Elvis stood up for him during his opening night show on September 3, 1973:

> *There's a guy here that works in the Italian restaurant. His name is Mario. And these people are getting ready to fire him as soon as I leave. And I don't want him to go. He needs the job. And I think the Hiltons [owner Conrad and son Barron] are greater than that. No disrespect. I just wanna wake up Conrad and tell him about Mario's job. That's all. This next song [Tiger Man] is dedicated to the hierarchy—the staff of the Hilton Hotel. [Elvis sings, "I'm the king of the jungle. They call me the Tiger Man."]*

Elvis often introduced his karate instructor and close friend Ed Parker:

> *I'd like you to meet one of the fellows who promoted me to the 8th degree black. His name is Ed Parker. He has about eighteen kenpo schools around the country. Ed Parker.*

> *The guy I gave the belt to is a good friend of mine. He's my karate instructor. Ed Parker.*

On September 2, 1974, during Elvis's Las Vegas show, he shared an incident about the time comedian Jerry Lewis pulled up beside his Rolls Royce:

> *Jerry Lewis—you know what he did one time. This is the truth. When I first got out of the army in 1960, I bought a*

> Rolls Royce. I was driving it in Beverly Hills one day, and
> Jerry Lewis pulled up beside me. He looked over at my car,
> and I did the same thing. He called my manager [Colonel
> Parker] that same day to say: "Tell Elvis not to drive a Rolls
> Royce without a tie." Swear to God! Well, I'll give you a
> couple of guesses as to the message I sent back. The next
> day I was driving it naked as a jaybird.

Singer and songwriter Neil Diamond was in the crowd of one of
Elvis's 1970s appearances:

> In the audience, ladies and gentlemen, is a great songwriter
> and a heck of a performer. He's a heck of a nice guy. He
> wrote Sweet Caroline. He wrote Holly Holy. I'd like you
> to say hello to Mr. Neil Diamond. Neil—you out there?
> Finally found you with the spotlight. Thanks for coming in.
> Thank you for coming in.

Singer Vikki Carr was in the audience of Elvis's Las Vegas show
on September 2, 1974:

> There's a lady in the audience I'd like to introduce you to.
> She's been in to see my show twice before. The reason we
> have a mutual respect is because the only way we know
> how to sing is from the gut out—both of us. You know
> who I'm talkin' about—her name is Vikki Carr.

Singer Wayne Newton was in the audience of one of Elvis's
1970s Las Vegas shows:

> Wayne Newton. Is he in here? Wayne, where are you?
> Stand up, son. Sit down Wayne.

The Rock group Led Zeppelin attended Elvis's concert at the
Los Angeles Forum on May 11, 1974:

> We got Led Zeppelin out there.

Actor Ernest Borgnine and actress Ann-Margret were in the audience of Elvis's Las Vegas show on February 23, 1973:

A gentleman I've known for a long time, one of the nicest men I've ever met, and one of the finest actors, Mr. Ernest Borgnine.

The girl that opens here tomorrow night, and believe me, ladies and gentlemen [applause]—let me finish, we made a movie together called Viva Las Vegas. Anyway, since then, she has developed one of the greatest stage acts you've ever seen. I'd like you to please say hello to Ann-Margret. Turn the light on her. You're beautiful. Put the light on her, man, I want to look at her. Thank you, dear. And I got a note here that says Colonel Parker is outside selling Ann-Margret's pictures.

On December 4, 1976, in Las Vegas, Elvis introduced singers Engelbert Humperdinck and Roy Orbison to his fans:

There's a couple of people in the audience I'd like for you to meet. I know you'd like to see them. They're some of the finest singers in the world, so that's one of the reasons I have to be good. I'm being judged, not only by you and the people on stage, but by them. You remember the song, Please Release Me, Let Me Go? Well, nobody ever sung it like Engelbert Humperdinck. And next to him, ladies and gentlemen, another one of the finest singers of all time—Roy Orbison.

Elvis's policeman friend John O'Grady was in the audience of his Las Vegas show on September 2, 1974:

There's another fellow in the audience—let me see that book—that's a friend of mine. His name is John O'Grady. He's written a book. He was head of the narco squad in

Holly-Las Vegas for twenty-six years . . . If you like things like The French Connection—*if you like that type stuff, buy this book. It's called* O'Grady. *It will fascinate you. It's about twenty-six years of a hard-line policeman working in the narco squad out of Hollywood, so you can imagine what it's like. Buy this book, it's called* O'Grady.

Renowned animal trainer Gunther Gebel-Williams was in the audience of Elvis's August 19, 1974, Las Vegas show:

There's a gentleman in the audience I'd like for you to meet, ladies and gentlemen. He's been with the Barnum and Bailey circus for a long time. He's one of the greatest animal trainers in the world. I mean, this cat gets in the ring with like twelve tigers and seven lions and everything, and I sleep with that every night, but you know, uh [laughter], naw. All kidding aside, he's a very nice, good friend of mine. His name is Gunther Gebel-Williams. Gunther, stand up and let them see you. Stand up.

During his May 27, 1974, Sahara Tahoe, Nevada, show Elvis introduced his mentor, Billy Eckstine:

There's a gentleman in the audience I'd like you to meet. First of all, I gotta tell you a little story. When I was in school, this man was one of the biggest inspirations of my life—as far as singing. And he's performing here in town now. And it's a pleasure to introduce—I gotta tell you something else. The high collars—he originated them twenty years ago—Billy Eckstine. Billy—outta sight. Thank you for coming in. It's really a pleasure, man, thank you.

On March 24, 1956, Robert Brown interviews Elvis and asks the young star for the names of his favorite singers:

I like Sonny James—Oh, I couldn't mention all of 'em.

Frank Sinatra, I like—I like Mario Lanza.

Elvis disclosed his passion for performing in front of his fans during a press conference held in Houston, Texas, in 1970:

> *Well, I think the most important thing is the inspiration that I get from a live audience. I was missing that. I enjoy it. I know I'm going to enjoy it here, because it's a live audience. It makes a world of difference.*

Unlike a lot of performers, Elvis loved to talk and interact with his fans. Some fans' most treasured memories are those words he spoke to them:

> *I want to tell you a little bit about this jewelry that I got on. No, this thing I wore on the Hawaii special. You know, people thought it was one big stone, and it's not. It's eleven-carat stone, which is pretty big, you know. It's as big as I've ever seen. Next to Elizabeth's [Elizabeth Taylor's]. I think she's got the biggest ones. I think you're right. The biggest diamond, too [laughs]. You're fast. You're good, boy. This thing here I had designed for the stage. It's got all different shapes of diamonds. It's for the stage. This I got tonight for you. You know, really, I just got it tonight. The reason I'm telling you this is because I think you ought to know. You helped pay for them [laughs].*

Elvis was always candid with his fans. If he was nervous, he would admit it, as he did at his January 28, 1971, show in Las Vegas:

> *If I appear shaky, it's because I'm a little shaky.*

Elvis praised his audiences for their responsiveness as he did during this 1970s concert:

Thank you very much. Oh, you are out of sight. You are fantastic. Boy, I tell you what. I couldn't have got a better audience if I stood out there and paid everybody twenty dollars to come in here. I really couldn't. You are out of sight, boy.

During an *American Bandstand* anniversary show, in a phone interview with Dick Clark, Elvis talks about his German fans:

I get along real well. Every day when I finish work and come in, there are a lot of people at the gate—from all over Germany, you know—and they bring their families. Especially on weekends, I have a lot of visitors here from all over Germany—from all over Europe in fact. They come here, you know, and bring pictures and take pictures.

His fans brought him gifts at his concerts:

You're trying to bribe me with those flowers, aren't you. It works. I'll be over there in a minute.

Elvis jokes with his fans during a Fort Worth, Texas, performance in 1974:

[Female fan screams] After the show, honey.

[Looking up in the balcony during the same show] Those binoculars look like a bunch of frogs.

Elvis loved his fans and cautioned them not to get hurt:

Honey, don't you jump out of that balcony and don't lose anything, either.

Elvis in action—note guitar pick in his left hand

Just be careful. We don't want anyone to fall down and get hurt, you know. That's all.

~

I've got to tell you folks something—for everybody that got kissed. I kissed somebody last night, and I caught their creeping crud, and if I got it—if I got it, you got it.

Elvis treated his fans with respect and compassion:

Hope you have a good time this evening. We're going to do a lot of songs and walk around and kiss people [Girl screams]. So, just relax and enjoy yourself, and we're going to do something to make you happy.

~

She says, "Kiss me one or I'll die." So, I can't let her die.

Elvis was loyal to his fans. [If we were as loyal to our clients we would be a success too.] He expressed his gratitude to his fans during a 1956 interview:

I just wish there was some way to go 'round to every one of 'em and really show that you appreciate their liking you and all. But that's impossible, really. I mean, lots of times if I'm in a crowd at the door, and the people who hired us are wanting the crowd to leave . . . maybe the people want to close up the auditorium. It makes me feel real bad because I can't get to all of 'em.

During his last Las Vegas engagement at the Hilton Hotel in December 1976, Elvis sprained his ankle, and it made it difficult for him to perform.

The first record I recorded was called That's All Right, Mama, *and gosh, it was at least three or four years ago. At least that. But, anyway the only thing we had was a rhythm guitar, an electric guitar, and an upright bass and a shaky leg. But I'd like to do that song, you know. It don't make no sense. The words are crazy, but you know nothing does tonight [laughs]. Except you people showing up. You know, that's fantastic. I would've come out here—I would have come down here, really, if I had to do it from a wheelchair. I swear to God.*

During a 1962 interview, Elvis talks about selecting his friends:

I don't try to surround myself with a group of intellectuals. It's more important to try to surround yourself with people who can give you a little happiness—because you only pass through this life once. You don't come back for an encore.

There are men who—in so many words, they're phony. There are men who knock you behind your back and then they're your buddy to your face. I like a man who's pretty much the same all the time—is pretty straight. He's himself to a certain extent. Now you can surround yourself with intellectuals or people of your so-called equal, and you can have dissension. There can be a jealousy there, and that's bad. The only thing you can learn there is to become bitter, and envy and everything else.

I learn from people. I learn from the people I work with. I learn from everyday life itself—being connected with a lot of different people. You can be fooled by having a group of people around you. Think you're learning something from and you're not learning a damned thing. You're not benefiting anything from it. I had a girl tell me one night, "Don't make the mistake, Elvis, of surrounding yourself with people you can't learn something from [implying his friends]," and the girl never caught it, but I got up and walked away from her. I smiled and walked away. I never said a word,

but in so many words I was saying, I can't learn anything from you [laughs].

Elvis sent a special message to his fans in the United Kingdom in 1964:

Well hello, everybody, this is Elvis. I'm sorry I can't be with you all for the New Musical Express Concert. But I'd like to congratulate all the winners, and I'd like to thank you for including me. I'm especially proud of all my friends in Great Britain, and I hope to be able to bring you the kind of songs and pictures that you like. So again, thanks from the bottom of my heart. I send my best wishes for your good health and happiness always. I'd like to wish the Beatles much continued success, as well as the other great recording artists in England. Thank you.

Years later, Elvis discussed his desire to tour outside of the United States:

Uh, just tell them I really love their devotion and that we're going to come see them. We got to. I've been saying it for years, but we will.

During a Las Vegas press conference in 1972, announcing his "Aloha from Hawaii" television special, Elvis was asked if he was going to tour Japan:

As far as a personal appearance, I don't have a definite time, but I would like to come over there. I would like to go to Japan.

Elvis was asked how he felt about his Japanese fans that came to the states to see him:

[Smiles] I love 'em.

Elvis appreciated his fans' enthusiastic response to his shows:

Thank you. You're a fantastic audience. I love you.

Tickle Me

(Elvis on Humor)

In the late 1980s some people claimed that Elvis faked his death. When Elvis returned to live performances in Las Vegas in 1969, he made this joke:

> *This is my first live appearance in nine years. I appeared dead a few times [laughs].*

Elvis loved to joke with his fans and bandmates:

> *Before I do anything else, I'd like to introduce the members of my band. Charlie [rhythm guitarist], this is Jerry [bass player]. Uh, now that they know each other we can go on with the show [laughs].*

During his August 15, 1969, Las Vegas show Elvis talked about meeting his manager Colonel Parker:

> *And then I met Colonel Sanders, uh Parker [laughs].*

During a rehearsal for the 1972 documentary *Elvis on Tour*, Elvis is asked where he would like to place the song *Burning Love* in the show:

> *[He gasps] Yo, shit, where would we put it! "Shoot," excuse me, sound fellow. I keep forgettin' [he was being recorded]. Doo-doo, where would we put it! [laughs] A thirty-seven-year-old man sayin' doo-doo. [laughs]*

Elvis joked with his fans during a Las Vegas show in 1969:

> *They're going to put me away, man. I know it's just a matter of time, boy.*

As he observed fans holding binoculars at Municipal Coliseum in Portland, Oregon, on November 11, 1970:

> *Those binoculars look like a bunch of frogs up there.*

Elvis joked with his fans during a 1974 concert series in Fort Worth, Texas:

> *I'm going to stand here in front of fourteen thousand people and laugh my career away.*

> *I'd like to walk around and get my breath back. Have you seen my breath over there?*

Elvis often introduced himself as another performer to break the ice with his audiences:

> *Good evening, ladies and gentlemen. Welcome to the International. My name is B. B. King. (1970s concert)*

> *Good evening, ladies and gentlemen. My name is Glen Campbell. [Laughter] Would you believe Wayne Newton? (Los Angeles, California, on May 11, 1974)*

> *Good evening, ladies and gentlemen. My name is Johnny Cash. (Portland, Oregon: November 11, 1970)*

> *Good evening. My name is Pat Boone. (Sahara Tahoe, May 24, 1974)*

Good evening. My name is Sammy Davis. (Sahara Tahoe, May 27, 1974)

One evening at the International Hotel, Elvis welcomed his fans by saying:

Good evening, ladies and gentlemen. Welcome to the Golden Nugget.

In Las Vegas, performers' mouths would easily dry out due to the climate. Elvis made the following joke many times while performing there:

My mouth feels like Bob Dylan slept in it or something.

During a 1974 concert Elvis joked:

I got a couple of people in the audience I'd like to say hello to. Hello, couple of people in the audience.

Elvis drank a lot of Gatorade during his shows:

I've got some Gatorade in case my gator needs aid.

Elvis would oftentimes say he recorded a song years before he had:

That's All Right—that was one of the first records I made—back in 1927, I think it was [it was actually recorded in 1954].

Before singing one of his hits Elvis often said:

This is one of my biggest records. Actually it was no bigger than the rest of them. They were all about the same size, but it sounds impressive.

When introducing the song *Hound Dog*, Elvis would say he would get into a girl's face and look her square in the eye:

Elvis in his blue swirl jumpsuit in 1974

I looked her square in the eye, because that's all she had was one square eye.

During a 1972 Las Vegas show, Elvis noticed a bug running across the stage while he was introducing the song *Hound Dog*:

There's a bug that went across the floor. He's moving out, boy. [Laughter] Any of you guys had any problems or anything? [Laughter] Says he's a bass singer. [Laughter]

At the Louisiana Hayride in 1955, Elvis introduced his first record:

Friends, we're too pooped to pop. Here's a little song that we always like to do. But it's the one that got me on my way in this racket, in this business. It's the first record I ever made [That's All Right].

Closing a 1950s show:

I'd like to stay out here and shake, rattle and roll for you all night, but we're booked in Alcatraz tomorrow night.

Talking to his audience:

All seriousness aside.

While kissing girls during his show, Elvis would quip:

Tough way to make a living, boys.

During one 1970s concert someone threw some things on stage and got Elvis's attention:

What are you throwing down here? What is that? No Doz [caffeine tablets]. We look like we're asleep up here? What's the matter with you?

During his August 10, 1970, Las Vegas show there was a feedback sound that resembled the sound of the intercom system used on the television show *Star Trek*:

[Feedback] Yes, Kirk. [Laughter]

Elvis introduced his song *I'm Leavin'* to a Boston, Massachusetts, crowd on November 10, 1971:

> *I have a record out called,* I'm Leavin'. *I'm not going to sing it—I'm just going to do it. I'm arriving.*

Humor was one technique that Elvis used to keep himself, his employees, and fans interested in his music. Since most of his Las Vegas audiences were adults, Elvis sometimes made off-color remarks or playfully altered the lyrics of songs:

> *[During singing of* Yesterday*] Oh, I believe in yesterday . . . Suddenly, I'm not half the stud [laughs] I used to be. (International Hotel; opening night; July 31, 1969)*

◞◞◞

> *[During singing of* Don't Be Cruel*] Baby if I made you mad for something I might have said, please forget the past before I kick your . . . [cymbal crash] (August 26, 1969)*

◞◞◞

> *[During singing of* Jailhouse Rock*] The band was jumping and the joint began to swing, you should've heard those knocked-out sons of bitches sing. (August 26, 1969)*

◞◞◞

> *[During singing of* Trying To Get To You*] I've been traveling night and day—I've been streaking all the way—baby, trying to get to you.*

◞◞◞

> *[During several attempts at singing* Bridge Over Troubled Water *Elvis gets tickled] It's a serious song, Glen D. (piano player). Straighten up and fly right. I'm straight. You all are*

crazy. It's a real beautiful song called Love Me Tender. *Bridge Over River Kwai.*

Elvis also made recording sessions and rehearsals fun for his fellow musicians:

> *[During take of* U.S. Male*] She's wearing a ring I brought [instead of "bought"] her [laughs]—ah, you fucked up, U.S. Male [laughs]. (RCA Studios; Nashville, Tennessee, January 17, 1968) [Someone tells Elvis if he could do two or more takes like that then he'd have a complete party album, and everyone laughs.]*

> *[During singing of* Love Me*] If you ever go, darling, I'll be oh so—horny [laughs]. (rehearsal in Culver City, California, July 16, 1970)*

> *[During singing of* The Next Step Is Love*] . . .and the next step is sex—the next step is love. (1970 Las Vegas rehearsal)*

While in the studio recording the song *Bringing It Back* on March 2, 1975, at RCA's Hollywood studios, the piano player hit the wrong key at the beginning of the song. Elvis quipped:

> *Next piano player. [laughs]*

Elvis gets perturbed about distractions while recording a live album at Graceland for RCA records in 1976:

> *[Telephone rings.] Damn telephone. Turn that thing off. Shoot it off the wall. Pardon the expression, "shoot it off the wall." [They begin take four of* Bitter They Are, Harder They Fall *and a dog barks (Laughter)]. Shoot the dogs and the phone. Hold it. Shoot the yellow dog. [Laughter] I'll be*

> *damned if Getlo [Elvis's deceased dog] didn't show up,*
> *didn't he?*

While recording the standard *Until It's Time for You to Go*, Elvis
changed the lyrics to say:

> *You're not a dream, you're not an angel, you're a woman.*
> *Lord I hope so, Lord . . .*

Hard Knocks

(Elvis on Sports)

Elvis was very active. He loved to participate in sports. It was a release for him. It was his way of relaxing. Football was Elvis's favorite team sport. He tried out for the team at L. C. Humes High School in Memphis, Tennessee. He later sponsored his own touch football team, and the jerseys said E. P. Enterprises. Elvis and his entourage played football during breaks while filming his movies. His favorite professional team was the Cleveland Browns. In his 1962 Jack Bentley interview, Elvis spoke of the game:

> I wanted to play football. I have a great ambition to play football—I have had and I still have, believe it or not. I've got a touch league—a touch football league back home. I would say right now, all kidding aside; the thing I keep up with most is professional football. I know all the players. I know all their numbers—who they play for. I've had people quiz me on it. That's a big thing with me right now. I watch all the games that I can. I get the films from the teams themselves if I can.

He talks about other sports:

> I like rugged sports. I'm not knocking people who like golf and tennis and the other things, but I like rugged sports, such as boxing, football, and karate and things like that.

During a 1956 interview, Elvis discussed what he liked to do with his leisure time:

> *When I do get some time off, I usually—I always go home and see my folks, and oh I ride a motorcycle and do different things. I do a little water skiing, and I like football; I like boxing.*

During a September 15, 1972, press conference he comments on how he paces himself:

> *I exercise every day. I vocalize every day. I practice if I'm working or not. So, I just try to stay in shape all the time—vocally and mentally. Both is tough. You gotta work at 'em, but I don't mind it, you know. It's worth it.*

Elvis began taking karate lessons while stationed in Germany, and he continued over the following years with a number of teachers in a variety of styles, reaching the rank of 8th degree black belt. He is credited with introducing the sport to much of the public by using karate in his movies. Elvis also used karate in a dance sequence in his 1968 NBC-TV special and he

Elvis's Kenpo Karate Gi

incorporated it into his concerts. During his September 28, 1974, concert at College Park, Maryland, Elvis shared his interest in karate with his audience:

> You may or may not know I study the art of karate. All right. Okay. Well, three weeks ago, I was given the 8th degree black belt. I've been doing it for sixteen years. [Applause] Thank you . . . I've had five different instructors in five different styles. So anyway, let me tell you what happened to old showoff here. You know, I've got policemen up on my floor, so I was hitting the wall— showing them how to hit. All right, I didn't hit it just once. I hit it about fifteen times. I hit it with that little finger and broke it. I mean I broke that little finger, you know. [Crowd gasps an 'ahhh.] I didn't break it. I'm lying. You are all 'ahing' for nothing.

At another Las Vegas show on August 30, 1974, Elvis explained his love for the art of karate:

> There are a lot of people who know that I have been involved in the art of karate for some time, but nobody knows to what degree, or whatever . . . kung fu and karate are the same thing. There's no difference, just the Chinese terminology uses kung-fu and the Japanese uses karate. The word "kara" means "open hand" . . . I mean "open," "te" means "hand," karate. See, I've been doing it every day of my life ever since, for at least two to three to six hours a day. And it's been tremendous for me as far as body conditioning, mind control, weight control, breathing techniques. It involves yoga. It involves meditation. There's a lot to it. It's not just breaking boards and fighting . . . So anyway I've been doing it for sixteen years, and practicing it, and I've never had to use it in my life in a violent way. And it's not for that reason, you see. On the contrary, it gives you a little more self-confidence. It makes you a little better citizen in your daily life . . . So anyway I got my first

black belt in 1960. I tested five hours for it. I had to fight two guys, one a fourth-degree black belt and one a black, had to fight 'em both at once, and then separately. [laughs] And they just beat the daylights outta me, I mean. But, it was part of the training. The highest degree in karate is the red belt. A lot of people don't know that. The 8th, 9th, and 10th degree red belt . . . This one, [referring to the belt he had] this tab, is Associate Master of the Art. The 8th . . . there's only ten, remember—this I got three days ago, this carries the title of Master of the Art. [Applause] Thank you very much. I hope I didn't bore you at all. I didn't mean to do that. [Applause] Thank you very much.

Elvis's stepbrother David Stanley received his 1st degree black belt from Elvis on March 3, 1976. Note Elvis's signature.

In 1971 Elvis wrote the TCB [Taking Care of Business was his personal philosophy for life] Oath during a flight from Los Angeles to Memphis:

The TCB Oath

More self-respect, more respect for fellow man.
Respect for fellow students and instructors.
Respect for all styles and techniques.
Body conditioning, mental conditioning, meditation
for calming and stilling of the mind and body.
Sharpen your skills, increase mental awareness for all
Those who might choose a new outlook and personal
Philosophy.
Freedom from constipation.

TCB TECHNIQUE

All techniques into one

Elvis Presley, 8th [karate rank]

Applying all techniques into one.

In the mid-1970s Elvis designed his own karate patch. It was round and included his TCB and lightning bolt emblem centered at the top. It had seven stars that represented God's perfect number and included the words Faith, Spirit, and Discipline. The black background represented the heavens, the white represented purity and red was symbolic of the blood of Christ.

On February 18, 1974, during Elvis's midnight show in Las Vegas, four men staggered onto the stage, brandishing fists. Elvis used a karate move and knocked one assailant off the stage onto a table. Bodyguards Red West, Sonny West, and Jerry Schilling, plus bass player Jerry Scheff took care of the rest. It turned out that all the assailants had police records and knew karate. As security led the men out, fans grabbed at them and struck them. Elvis had a few choice words:

> I'm sorry, ladies and gentlemen. I'm sorry I didn't break his goddamn neck. You want to shake my hand, that's fine. If he's going to get tough, whup his ass.

During his early career, Elvis would sometimes find himself involved in scuffles in self-defense. Here Elvis responds to a newspaper story involving a 1957 fight:

> Well, it's just a case of get them or be got. [laughs] Somebody hittin' me or trying to hit me. I mean, I can take ridicule and slander, and I've been called names, you know. Right to my face and everything. That I can take. But I've had a few guys that tried to take a swing at me, and naturally, you can't just stand there. You have to do something.

Elvis came up with the idea for his stage costumes from the karate gi [outfit]. During a 1970 press conference at the Houston Astrodome, he was asked about the outfits he wears:

> I got the idea from a karate suit, because I've studied karate for a long time and I had them make up a couple of suits like it.

Elvis was later asked what he did for relaxation:

> Karate. [laughs] If you can relax doing this. [Does karate moves with his hands.] I don't know. No, I read a lot and go horseback riding and stuff like that.

Bibliography

Coffey, Frank. *The Complete Idiot's Guide to Elvis*. New York: Alpha Books, 1997.

Cotton, Lee. *All Shook Up*. Ann Arbor: Popular Culture, Inc., 1993.

Guralnick, Peter, and Jorgensen, Ernst. *Elvis—Day By Day*. New York: Ballantine Books, 1999.

Pierce, Patricia. *The Ultimate Elvis*. New York: Simon and Schuster, 1994.

Presley, Elvis. *Elvis Answers Back*. Lawndale, CA: Sound Publishing Corp., 1956.

Stanley, David. *The Elvis Encyclopedia*. Santa Monica, CA: General Publishing Group, 1994.

Stern, Jane and Michael. *Elvis World*. New York: Alfred A. Knopf, Inc., 1987.

Worth, Fred, and Tamerius, Steve. *Elvis—His Life from A to Z*. Chicago: Contemporary Books, 1988.

Membership Application

You are cordially invited to join the Taking Care of Business Elvis Style Fan Club. We are dedicated to preserving and promoting the memory and image of Elvis Presley in a positive and respectful manner. We are a nonprofit, charity oriented club officially recognized and registered by the Estate of Elvis Presley.

As a member, you will receive quarterly newsletters, a membership card, and a few other surprises throughout the year. Our Club has personal contact with many Elvis family members and friends. I will provide all the latest news and information about Elvis and Elvis-related activities reported directly from Graceland, and other sources throughout the world.

Please mail all fan club correspondence to Taking Care of Business Elvis Style Fan Club, P.O. Box 671, Hurst, TX 76053. Membership dues are $15.00 per year in the U.S. and $20.00 per year outside the U.S. Please make your check or money order payable to Taking Care of Business Elvis Style Fan Club. Thank You.

Thank you for joining us in our effort to keep Elvis's memory alive.

Sincerely yours,

John Dawson
President

Name_____

Address_____

City_____   State_____   Zip_____

Home phone_____   Work phone_____

Fax number_____

E-mail_____

Birthday_____   Age_____

Quick Order Form

Fax Orders : 817-282-7725   Send this form.

Telephone Orders: 817-282-5889. Have your credit card ready.

Postal Orders: John Dawson, P.O. Box 671, Hurst, TX 76053. USA.
Telephone: 817-282-5889

E-mail Orders: john@dailydosesofhypnosis.com

Please send the following books at $19.95 each plus shipping. Texas orders add 8.25% sales tax.

Qty _____   *The Ways of Elvis*

Please send more **FREE** information on:
    Speaking/Seminars   Mailing Lists   Consulting

Name:_____

Address:_____

City_____State_____Zip_____

Telephone: _____

e-mail address: _____

Sales Tax: Please add 8.25% for products shipped to Texas addresses.

Shipping: Please add US $4 for the first book and $2.00 for each additional book.   International: US $9 for the first book and $5.00 for each additional book (estimate),

Payment : US checks made payable to John Dawson
Credit Card:
Visa   Mastercard   Amex   Discover

Card Number_____

Name on the Card_____

Expiration date _____